A Hound in the House

A Hound in the House

Chris Dignam

A Hound in the House

Published July 2013 by

Crafty Dog Books,

Ti Levran,

59 Capel Road, Clydach,

Swansea, UK. SA6 5PY

www.crafty-dog-cymru.co.uk

ISBN 978-0-9576932-0-3

Designed & Typeset by Crafty Dog Books

Printed in Great Britain by MWL Printing ,

New Inn, Pontypool,

Torfaen, Wales, UK

…

All photographs by Chris Dignam

© Chris Dignam

Jacket illustrations by Jackie Evans/Jacs Studio

© Jackie Evans/Jacs Studio

www.jacslittlewelshstudio.co.uk

iv

Dedication

This book is dedicated to Armelle, my very dear and patient wife, and to my Mam and Dad who got me my first dog way back in the mists of time.

It is also dedicated to all those involved in animal rescue and greyhound rescue in particular, and especially to Sally, Sammy and Penny, without whom this work would not have come about.

"You cannot fatten a Greyhound." D.I. Evans, attrib.

Prologue

A Hound in the House

The following is a cross - a mongrel, if you like — between a guide to owning a rescue dog and the joys and trials of being a pet owner. The joys by far out-weigh the trials. It is not the definitive guide to either rescuing or to greyhounds but as we found out ourselves, all information is useful when you start out. Hopefully you will either read this and think, "Oh, that's what we did", or "Our dog was like that" or better still will encourage you to go out and re-home a rescue dog (or cat, or hamster, or....). But most of you reading this will already have a rescued greyhound sitting next to you (or on top of you) as you read this. It began as a short tale (tail??) about one dog, but the mania encompassed a few more, each one a real personality in their own right.

Chris Dignam, January 2013

Contents

Why a Greyhound?

I had never really been interested in Greyhounds. When I was a kid I had a dog who was my best friend when growing up. After my wife Armelle and I got together we had often "borrowed" family dogs over the years. It was a treat both for us and for them for a few weeks a year – all had been large dogs, Old English sheepdogs, Briards - spoiling them rotten until they went home after their holidays. I suppose you could say that dogs ran in our family (though not "running" dogs!).

My wife had gone part-time at work and I got a job only 20 minutes from home which meant that a dog would not be left alone all day, so having a dog would be viable. We then began to wonder what breed of dog to have. Old English? Too big, too much maintenance. Briard – too expensive, and should we really just line a breeder's pocket? Maybe a rescue dog? That would help get a dog out of a pound, and give a poor dog a home. That sounded morally acceptable. Then, "What about a rescued greyhound? They have a horrible life," became the tone of the conversation at home. Like I said, I had never really considered greyhounds.

Someone in work reminded me that a colleague was involved in Greyhound Rescue. Linda – the colleague in question – told me a bit more about it, gave me some contact names and I took it from there. Apparently the Greyhound Rescue group she was involved with took dogs from the South Wales tracks or from Ireland. They had dogs across the area in rented kennels or in "foster" homes. When a dog was taken in they usually went into a kennels but they would need to be assessed as to their temperament, how they behaved, whether they were housetrained, how they got on with people, small dogs or cats. This could best be done by taking the dog into a real home, to spend time with a family and see how they adjust. This is an important part of the adoption process as it gives the adopter a better view of the dog, and helps to match adopter and adoptee.

Prior to our "house visit" there was a panic over whether to clean the house or to leave it "lived in" (I can't remember what we eventually decided but it was probably to leave the "lived in" look). The couple who came to "vet" us arrived with a surprise visitor; we had our first meeting with a greyhound face to face. His name was Oddjob and he arrived with his owners Pauline and Rob. He was a mostly black dog, tall, thin but muscley – what in an American novel would be termed "rangy". The obvious question was "Why Oddjob?" He was christened this because when he had been in his foster home he had been clean but left a "present" on his first time alone.

My wife as I said before was already sold on the idea of a rescue greyhound; after meeting Oddjob, I too was sold. (OK - Cliché time) - If any dog could be noble, then this dog was. He was quiet, a strong silence with eyes which looked so very sad and deep. As he sat there you could imagine his forbears lying at the feet of ancient kings and lords in castles and palaces. However, his was not such a noble tale; it was a sad story of abuse, neglect but eventual rescue and release.

Some dogs are with their foster parents a short time whilst others never leave; these foster parents, I found out later, had four dogs that arrived, found a niche and never left. Imagine bringing in an emaciated, beaten, frightened bag of bones and then bringing it back to become a settled, more confident bundle of muscles, legs and licky tongue. Once you build that initial bond it is difficult to break it. But what about a dog of our own? We passed the home check - another hurdle over – one step closer to re-homing a dog.

There was much frantic Internet searching for information on coping with a rescued dog and what to expect when you get them home. Websites were scoured, notes taken and a scrapbook compiled. Armed with this and new-found confidence the following Bank Holiday Monday found us ("us" being my wife and I and our young nephew John) arriving late, as usual, skidding into the Greyhound Rescue Show at Pembrey Country Park just as people were starting to leave. Rob and Pauline and Lynda pointed out two prospective dogs. Fortunately for them but not for us, one, a black dog, had been homed that week.

Another dog standing with two children caught my eye. She was tall, taller than most of the other greyhounds we had seen, white and fawn - like a Jack Russell on stilts and steroids. She was "smiling" broadly, a yellow bow hung

4

loosely around her neck, pushed to one side by her head's perpetual swivel to watch the action all around her. This was that other dog; her name was Sally but, well, we were warned, she was a bit boisterous. You could see how excitable she was.

Game for anything by this stage, I took her lead and we set off across the park. She allowed me to lead her as if we had been together for years - greyhounds are usually lead trained and walk well as they are used to being taken out in groups by the kennel hands at the track. As the four of us walked I could see that it was not just me that had fallen for Sally - Armelle was clearly besotted. What really clinched it was the way that Sally allowed John to cuddle her, fuss her and to take her on the lead. Consider that we were all new to her, there was so much going on around her and John was squeezing her like a vice. She accepted it all without a murmur. We walked her back to the cars and then had a glimpse of that boisterous nature – two loose dogs were running a few hundred yards away across the park. Sally's eyes stuck out like organ stops, her ears were extended like galleons in full sail and her body tensed like a spring at full stretch. Then she did it

- she yowled a high-pitched tortured yowl and spun around as if trying to screw herself into the turf. I hung onto the lead for dear life but apart from the yowl and pirouette she made no attempt to escape. You can't beat your genes - three thousand years of breeding and track training do not disappear overnight. This "boisterous" outburst I supposed would also account for the dried blood on her cheek where she had become excited earlier in the day and had nipped her tongue! Still alert but calmer, we made our way back to our point of origin where Lynda, Pauline and Rob stood. As we talked I noticed that on Sally's right flank was a brown patch, about the size of an old ten pence piece where there was no skin and bare dark skin. I could not help but wonder what that was so made a mental note to ask when I got a chance.

That evening we talked and talked, discussing whether this dog would be the right one for us, should we wait for another dog…the discussion was endless and we went in circles like the electric hare. There was nothing for it but to have a proper "field test" so Sally came home for one day the following weekend as a trial. She travelled really well in the car, curious for the first few miles, watching the world go by but this soon got boring so she flaked out in the back of the car. At the house she was soooo quiet; polite, well behaved (though not understanding a word of command!) and the day went well, apart that is from a minor accident on the living room carpet and the fact that she came into season on our kitchen floor! But hey, these are the joys and responsibilities of being a dog owner. She was so quiet that we could not believe that this was a boisterous dog – after all, we were used to very big bouncy Briards – if this one was boisterous, the quiet ones must come with a wheelchair and a drip!

We took Sally back to Phillipa, her foster mother, and said that we would really like her to come home with us permanently. The problem was my having to go into Hospital for three days in three weeks time, which meant Phillipa would have to look after Sal for another four weeks. We felt certain that this would not be satisfactory and had begun to resign ourselves to waiting for another dog. It was, after all, a real imposition to ask Phillipa to house and feed her for another three weeks. What a brilliant person – she said that she would look after Sally, no problem, until we were ready.

We can never thank Phillipa enough for her patience, kindness and her very hard work. In fairness she had the hardest time with Sal; Sal was pretty clean but the final housetraining was done by Phillipa, as well as Sal's getting fully used to being in a house day and night. What was revealing about Sally was something Phillipa told us when we collected her for the last time. The window in her kitchen has a Velux roof window. One day Phillipa when went to open the window with the window pole Sally cried out and flew across the room to the furthest corner where she huddled, cowering and shaking. This had been enough to reduce Phillipa to tears and she sat with Sally for ages settling and reassuring her. What was equally distressing was the dog's fear that no matter how kind people were she was still going to be beaten. Sally had a fear of all sticks and umbrellas. Now we understood what the mark was on Sally's side – evidently one of her previous owners had not been anything like as kind as

Phillipa. Later our vet confirmed that it was a stab wound.

The week before finally bringing Sal home had been a frantic one of chasing about for dog beds, bowls, and blankets and reading up on greyhounds. Many of the American web sites provide invaluable information on what to expect, what you need to do and generally explaining how the dog views the new house. Expect a pool of wee, for example as the dog will feel insecure in a strange place and may have an accident which may be a way of making the house smell a bit familiar.

One of the recommendations was for a "martingale" collar, a form of nylon webbing choker specially made for sight hounds. Greyhounds and whippets have necks that taper which makes an ordinary collar useless. With an ordinary collar the dog will see something, you will feel a tug and turn to see a muscley backside and tail disappearing into the distance almost as fast as the cat it is chasing. Likewise, chain chokers can hurt the dog and cut into their necks. As I was later to find out, a greyhound's neck can be very delicate. Most greyhounds wear wide leather

9

collars but as we were to find with Sally, she could not sit comfortably or bend to eat with one on. So, a semi-loose wide banded webbing collar would be better. A lot of shop searching and web searching resulted in us buying a martingale collar from Austin, Texas. It was red, only $8 and arrived within a week.

Another old wives tale bandied about on the web is that Greyhounds do not moult (or "shed" as the Americans put it). Whilst this may be true in the US where many states have a settled climate all year round – it was not true in South Wales, however. Sally moulted in bucket loads, fine white fur, and a brush would not touch it. The American sites suggested using a grooming mitt, which is a sort of rubber glove covered with rubber blobs. I can thoroughly recommend it - it pulls out the short fur, which can then be shaken off the glove. This proved to be a favourite with the local sparrows who collected the lumps of brushed fur off the lawn to line their nests. It was good to see that we were doing our bit for sustainability and to support the local wildlife! I wonder how thermally efficient greyhound fur is?

The New Arrival

Sal eventually arrived the next Friday and settled in really quickly. To be honest she walked in through the front door and decided that was it; she was never going to leave. At first she slept at night in a dog crate borrowed from my brother (for his dog, not for him). This large cage (three feet long, two feet high and two feet wide) may look a bit cruel but you have to remember that these dogs are used to being kept in pens and many dogs feel more secure in the familiarity of a crate. It takes the place of the wolf's den in the primeval canine past. It is always a big test to leave a dog alone for the first time. Would we have separation anxiety, would she howl or tear the door apart, or would she mess the room. That night we settled her in her crate with some toys and an old jumper of mine and apart from one initial cry, she never made a sound. During the day we started leaving her for short periods (5 minutes) gradually building up to a few hours over the first few weeks. Gradually we began to leave the door open longer and longer, starting by only closing her when we were in work, and then leaving it open all the time.

Within five weeks the crate was gone and she was sleeping in the open kitchen.

Greyhounds like their comfort – these bony dogs need something soft under them. Most adopt a chair or settee but we were set that dog's belong on the floor and not on the furniture. The first night she climbed up on the chair in the living room but I tipped her off – she never tried to get on the chair again. For sleeping, Sally had a soft dog bed that she climbed into but this had to be supplemented by a duvet. Armelle and I priced dog duvets and decided instead to get her a single human duvet and used an old cover of ours. Sal found this to be most acceptable. It was folded in half and she managed to wrap it around her or else roll one end up to make a pillow when she watched T.V.. Oh yes, Sally loved the telly. This was the couch potato greyhound that we had read about. Any programmes would do, but she preferred animal programmes. "Due South" was a real favourite when we first had her, as was "The Magician's House" a few Christmases later (she was especially fascinated by the talking dog). "Walking with Dinosaurs" proved to a little bit scary. We could never watch Crufts as she went absolutely loopy when the fly-ball came on. She would bark, run up and down and bump the tv screen with her nose. She would even look behind the tv to see where the dogs were hiding.

We discovered that Sal was also a creature of habit. For the first year or so we had her, after our evening meal she would pick up her chew and walk into the living room. If her duvet or dog bed was not by the side of my chair she would lean forward, look me in the eye and "chomp" a few times and sometimes even bark. That was her signal for me to take her bed in. She would then curl up and sleep or else stretch out and watch T.V.. To solve the problem of having to carry her duvet into the living room we acquired a fleece small dog duvet (which belonged to my sister's toy poodle). Believe it or not, this fitted Sally rather well – which begs the question how enormous it must have been for my sister's Poodle, or maybe a greyhound can just curl up into a very small space.

For the first few months Sally did not know what a chew was for, or what toys were. You must remember that greyhounds are bred and raised to race and they have no real time to act

13

like normal puppies. She would occasionally do a "play bow" (a sort of canine curtsy which is the introduction to a play session) as if she was beginning to play but then almost immediately she would stop and sit down, as if she thought she was doing something that it was wrong. Gradually we encouraged her to play with a squeaky toy or her ball but it took ages. We became accustomed to her getting up, "chomping", picking up her ball and whizzing up and down the room like an express train. Five minutes maximum, then she'd flop for a sleep. Small room and large fast greyhound proved to be an interesting combination though. Braking to a halt just before the tiled kitchen floor actually created small patches of melted carpet. And that was why they call greyhounds 40 miles per hour couch potato.

We have a cricket pitch behind the house and one circuit on her lead in the morning and evening was usually enough to keep her fit and happy. This became our usual routine after breakfast but before I went to work. Every other day we went for a longer walk along the canal but this was usually enough to reduce her to a panting greyhound with a lolling tongue as she walked

home (she survived the 2002 Gnoll Greyhound
Rescue sponsored walk where we got lost and
walked 2 miles too far really well though she slept
for two days afterwards!). Don't forget that these
are retired athletes and do not require the
intensive exercise they had in the past – after you
retire from work, would you fancy doing the same
job for fun? She did like to have a run but she
could only be trusted when there were no other
dogs about. It's a stupid point to reiterate but
Greyhounds can run <u>very</u> fast and if she decided
to clear off there would be nothing I could do to
stop her (Greyhounds are very independently
minded and not as blindly obedient as some other
dogs). The other problem was her seeing dogs
running off their lead which sent her nuts though
her yowling and spinning did subside to
manageable levels. Even the week before she
died she was still able to raise a yowl as another
dog jumped and ran on the other side of the pitch.

Ah, but when she ran it really was a sight
to behold. There is nothing in the world as
beautiful as a greyhound running at full stretch in
the sunshine not for money or for reward but just
for the love of running. Truly amazing.

We soon discovered that Sally absolutely loved music. Friends of ours had a band that rehearsed in a hall nearby and Sally and I went along to watch and listen (they were called SOPHA but then became Riley and later split – very sad, what a waste of great talent). Greyhounds can appear a bit stand offish when it comes to people – you can call them and try to fuss them as much as you like but they will only react if <u>they</u> want to; it is almost cat-like. She absolutely loved the band and would insist on wandering over to each of them in turn for a fuss despite the music blasting. Something about show business I suppose…. the roar of the greasepaint and the smell of the crowd..! The first car we had when Sal arrived was a little Renault Clio which did not have a large enough hatchback for a tall greyhound, so she would lie or sit in the space in front of the parcel shelf with the back seat pushed forward. When she went in the car (which she particularly enjoyed) she took to sitting with her head on the rear parcel shelf between the speakers. At first we thought this was just to watch the traffic, but we noticed that when we put certain music on she would get up from her normal position stretched prone on the back seat and rest her head on the parcel shelf. We soon realised she would sit there to listen to the music she liked – she was partial to a bit of Billy Joel, Burton Cummings or Blackmore's Night. Her particular favourite however was the Latin number, Mambo Number nine (known in our house as Sally's song). Strange dog. She was also a critic - Sal knew what she disliked. One year there was a concert on the cricket pitch behind our house. She had been sitting in the living room watching TV but as soon as the music started (some chart stuff like Steps etc.) she got up and wandered out to sit on the garden path in the sunshine listening to it. She lay there for about an hour, but then the music changed. As the slide guitar and opening bars of "Achy breaky heart" started she was up the garden like a shot and back in to watch TV instead. She evidently did not like country music.

The most amazing information on rescue greyhounds can be found on the Internet. In particular Adopt a Greyhound, "A Breed Apart", Fast Friends and Greyhounddog.org – and many British Greyhound Rescue sites.

Apart from telling us about the non-moulting of Greyhounds (!) they did have lots of very useful information (this was in the early days of greyhound websites – today there are absolutely hundreds of useful sites about). Of particular use was information on how to treat your dog when she has been spayed. Common-sense information like not allowing her to run about for fourteen days, keeping her leashed when exercising, and not to be too frightened when she is sick and ill the night after the operation. This was particularly distressing, for the poor dog had been sick and had an accident in her bed – she could hardly stand due to the stitches and the anaesthetic. It was hard to see who was most upset, her or me. Had I not already been prepared for this I think that I would have panicked completely. It did look really terrible and she looked so distressed. By the next day she was up and about, although she had problems sitting down very gingerly and I had to help to lift her down as she had difficulty bending her legs. Do not let your dog run around for ten days or so it had said, and keep the dog leashed when exercising. Common sense – a friend's dog decided to have a run the day after her operation and jumped a small picket fence. The wound opened and was only held together by one stitch. The resulting trip back to the vets doubled the cost of the initial operation!

Greyhounds have very long and bony tails, capable of practically doing a 360-degree swipe, particularly suited to clearing a coffee table of everything on it – cups, vases, remote controls…... This whip like device can be an especial problem for a happy dog. One lunchtime I came home to let Sal out and, as she was very excited and rather happy (as usual), she wagged

19

her tail and caught the tip of it on the frame of the back door. I thought nothing of it until I started to find little brown streaks and specks on the kitchen units and the floor. I started wiping them but more appeared where I just wiped. I was puzzled until the penny dropped - I spent the next forty minutes cleaning these drips of greyhound blood from everywhere. The kitchen looked like a major crime scene! I patched the tail up with micropore tape and cotton wool and we went to the vets but it continued specking for a further two weeks (this injury is a well-known greyhound one and is called "Happy Tail"). We eventually settled for having the tail tip removed down to where there was more flesh and fur to protect it. Great but this produced another problem; how do you allow air to the wound but protect it from being banged and start up bleeding again? One of our vets had a brain wave; he cut the tip off a large syringe and attached it to a tape base at the end of her tail. Air could get in through the tip of the syringe but it cushioned the blow of anything Sally banged against. This was a brilliant idea but had one minor side-effect in that instead of a whip-like tail she now had a lethal weapon in the form of a club,

20

which she inadvertently used to chip plaster off the kitchen wall and to once give me a sideswipe that burst my lip! The tail healed very quickly and became as furry as any other greyhound's, though a little bit shorter.

Accident Prone?

Sally was a great dog but she did have a habit of having accidents. O.K., let's be honest, she was really accident prone. The tail was the first, but there were quite a few others. As I said before, she never chewed any food, it always went down whole (this was not entirely true, as perversely she would crunch individual peanuts or small pieces of crunchy bacon or kibble if given to her one at a time). This was probably due to being raised in groups where the fastest dog to eat got most food. All I can assume is that she may not have been fast on the track, but she was incredibly swift at meal times. The food that greyhounds are given when racing is usually soft, like thick soup. They were the lucky ones. At our local greyhound track before it was closed staff scavenged the bins for thrown sandwich crusts and offcuts to feed the dogs. Many greyhounds have bad teeth as they have never had the need to chew hard food. It is this chewing and crunching that helps to massage the gums and to scrape plaque and bits of detritus from the teeth and gums. Sally's lack of chewing meant that instead I had to brush her teeth a few times a week when I remembered. The rawhide chews helped but there is no real substitute for crunchy food. On one of our trips to the vet we were given special chunky dried food. "My spaniel is the same and does not chew anything so we gave him this," the vet said. "She will have to crunch it to swallow it." Sounded a good idea and well worth a try. That evening we gave Sally a few of these large round crunchy bites, similar in shape and size to a golf ball. We watched expectantly as she sniffed them, picked one up and crunched it up. Excellent – we gave her another one, which Sal licked and then…swallowed it whole. You could see the shape of it going down her gullet like she was a cartoon greyhound. In an effort to try to get her to chew we started giving her bone shaped crunchy biscuits. This seemed to work, but you had to be there to supervise her eating. One Saturday, as we ate our tea, I gave her one of these doggy bones biscuits, which Sally bit in half and swallowed. Within minutes she began to salivate and swallow, as if something was stuck in her throat. We rang the vet and within half an

23

hour we were in the surgery seeing the emergency vet. It appeared that she had managed to swallow the bone but it must have scraped her gullet on the way down, making it feel like there was still a bone there. She was given a steroid jab to ease the pain and reduce any swelling and an antibiotic and we were told to keep an eye on her. The swallowing reflex grew less and less that evening but just in case I spent the night on the settee with Sally's bed on the living room floor next to me. She was fine by morning and so, after breakfast, we went for a walk up to the local park. It was a lovely Autumn Sunday morning. At the Park there was an elderly gent with a Doberman pup about 18 months old. He asked whether I was letting Sal off her lead for a run. I said that I did not usually, but he suggested that they could run together and exercise each other. "Does yours come back?" I asked gingerly. "Yes," the man replied. "Good, then Sally will come back!"

It had rained overnight but the grass on the rugby pitch was mostly dry. I unclipped Sally's lead and off she went with the Doberman, barking and nipping at each other as they ran. It was

24

lovely to watch them play, frolicking and gambolling like two hyperactive lambs. I stood talking to the gentleman in the very middle of the pitch. As we spoke I could hear in the distance but coming closer the thundering of paws, but thought nothing of it. Suddenly I heard a thud and a winded cry. I turned to the left where the man had been standing but there was no-one there. I looked down and he was lying prone in the mud. I forgot that when Sally runs she did not always look where she was going. 30 kilos of greyhound at 40 mph is a lot of kinetic energy! The chap got to his feet. I was really apologetic but he confessed that the same thing had happened the year before with a Rottweiler and he had landed that time on the concrete. Sally stood about twenty feet away. You could see her mind whirring; she evidently worked out that this was not a good thing and that she might get a row. She looked at me, cried, and hobbled back to me, limping, paw raised as if to say that I should not shout and that she was hurt too! We made rather a hasty exit and I skulked as she limped back up the road to the house. Just as well Sally had had that steroid injection! I had always been careful of

Sally running off the leash in case she injured herself. What I had failed to anticipate was her injuring someone else…..or even me…

Trips to the 'Out of Hours' Vets became a fairly regular thing with Sal – at least twice a year! Like the time we were serving up dinner and a boiled potato rolled off the plate and off the worktop. Sal was by my side by the time it hit the floor and I could stop her. The red-hot potato was in her mouth and down her throat before you could say "Emergency Vets". She managed to burn her throat, and within half an hour we were at the vets where she had a jab and painkillers. Did she learn? Nope, neither did we. The same thing happened with a cooked sausage that rolled off the kitchen table a while later. That time we did not have to go to the vet. And that time we learnt, even if Sally did not.

We had a routine that if it was quiet on the cricket pitch behind the house Armelle would hold Sal and I would walk on a hundred yards and then Sal would be released and she would run to me. This gave Sal a blast and it was great to see her run, as she really enjoyed it. However, one sunny summer's evening, Armelle, Sally and I went to

Singleton Park in Swansea for a walk. After checking that the coast was clear and that there were no wandering dogs to distract her we decided to give Sal a run. Armelle held her and I walked off about a hundred yards away and waited. I held out a grape – a particular greyhound treat - and put the others back in a bag in my rear pocket. Sally launched herself towards me at a real rate of knots. She was coming slightly downhill like a rocket and she launched to clear a large damp patch on the grass in front of me. I waited, holding the grape out. She always ran past me and turned to come back for whatever reward I had. There are many warnings on the web pages not to let a greyhound run at a child and not to step out of the way at the last moment but to keep still – the dog will always run past. She was about twenty feet away and then…I don't remember anything apart from trying to get back up, wondering why I was on the floor, where my glasses had gone and where the bus had come from that had run me over. 30 kilos of muscle, bone and soppy greyhound had hit me at 40 mph, taking my legs from under me and I had landed heavily on my left shoulder. Sally ran over to me

27

and was by my side as, dazed, I slipped her lead back onto her collar. Armelle was running down the hill towards me. I pulled my glasses on and stood up. My arm, shoulder and head ached. Armelle was mortified that people had seen this pantomime. "You have mud on your face…. You have grass in your ear…" she said. I fumbled and pulled a lump of mud and churned grass out of my left ear as if to confirm that. I also now had a back pocket full of grape juice! (I later discovered that this had been a good thing, as grapes are not good for dogs). I staggered along and made my way back to the car and we drove home. By the next day the bruises were coming out – and I could hardly turn my neck. I saw my doctor who found the story very amusing (thanks for the support, Doc!). He said that I had torn the deltoid and pectoral muscles and damaged the shoulder bone at the top of the clavicle. I had also probably received a mild concussion. The doctor prescribed 600 mg ibuprofen, which eased the pain and reduced the swelling but instead by the weekend I had terrible stomach pains. This I put down to the ibuprofen, which I stopped. The bouts of pain continued until I was rushed into hospital with appendicitis! The important thing was that Sally was uninjured. Despite colliding and rolling head over heels her general fitness was such that she bounced back without a scratch.

Greyhounds and stairs were another bad combination. She got the knack of going up and down stairs slowly almost immediately she arrived. Within a day or so Sal had perused the whole house and decided she liked lying on our bed with her head on my pillow (!). She soon began to run up and down the stairs, launching herself like a kangaroo from the front hall. Imagine lots of flying spindly legs going like train pistons as she tried to get upstairs in front of you and round the corner onto the landing. It was all fine until the day she missed the top step and landed with a "grumph" in a heap on the landing. She was OK for an hour but then she developed a limp and she began to hobble pitifully around the house. The next day Sally was no better so off we went to the vet. Sal had grown to dislike the vets due to her regular and frequent visits. If they had had a car park, we would have had our own space…..when they redecorated they would ask us what colour we liked….. Bearing in mind that she had hobbled all day, she got out of the car without the merest hint of a limp. Going in to the vet's consulting room, Nick the vet said "Hello Sally. It's no use – I can see you've got a limp." There was no fooling our vet! It turned out to be a sprained shoulder and a bruised foot. The thing that upset Sally more was that she was grounded for a week; no walkies and definitely no running or going upstairs to the Big Bed. This was Friday. By Sunday, limp or no, she was getting stir crazy. Try explaining to a greyhound why she can't go for a walk. All that resulted was that instead of having her walking slowly outdoors on a lead we had a 40 mph bored dog bouncing up and down our cluttered living room, threatening to destroy table lamps and tellies. By Tuesday we had to walk her if only a little bit. By Friday she was fine but she still had to wait for another week before she could run properly. Even up to the last weeks we had her, when we came in from work every day she would run up and down the living room like a maniac for two minutes, have a cuddle, then settle on her bed.

Accidents…. Sal was lying on the bed one evening and when she moved there was a little wet patch. Fortunately she was lying on her blanket so there was no leakage. We put this down to her being overfull and we had not let her out. Over the next few weeks she had more leaks, and she did not seem to know that she was weeing. I took Sal to the vets and he diagnosed weak bladder muscles probably due to being spayed. The vet gave us a bottle of propalin which we were to put in her food, once at breakfast and once at teatime. We worked out the normal dose then gradually reduced it to see what was the minimum she needed – problem solved, Sally was leak free. Her hips gave her a bit of discomfort as she got older so she went on cod liver oil and on glucosamine syrup. When she got to 11 she had injections of cartrophen for her arthritis but only twice a year and they worked really well.

Curiosity and the Greyhound

When we first had her, Sally lacked confidence and was quite shy. This changed and she became a very outgoing, inquisitive dog. For the first year or so she would not push her way through even a part-opened door. However, she soon learnt to push open any door. Her favourite was getting up the stairs (two bounds from hall to landing) and pushing the bedroom door open. If the door was latched all you heard was a soft thud as she biffed her nose on a resistant door that wouldn't let her in. And thereby hang another couple of tales. She liked to lie on our bed and so we kept a fleece throw on the middle of it to stop her leaving hair on our duvet. This was not good enough for Sal – she liked to lie at the top of the bed with her head on my pillow. If the TV was on, even better. If she got upstairs at the weekend when Armelle was in bed she would lie resolutely in between the two of us, pushing Armelle with her backside to make room. She liked the pillow so much that she developed a new party trick. If I was sitting or lying in bed and she couldn't get to the pillow, she would lie at the foot of the bed and "talk". When you lean forward to see what the matter is, she would wriggle up the bed and in behind you. Checkmate – pillow captured by a greyhound!

One afternoon Armelle and I were busy in the garden, pottering about, mowing and weeding. Sal was asleep on the lawn when last we looked. As the afternoon drew on I looked again and Sal had disappeared. I asked Armelle if she had seen her and she suggested she had gone in the house. I looked through the kitchen window – no sign. I looked in through the window into the living room – again, no sign. I looked out to the front garden and the gate was shut but Sal was a big dog and could clear the front wall if she had wanted. Beginning to panic by now, I called Armelle and we went inside the house. There was no sign of Sally so we went upstairs to change as we would have to go and look for her. I pushed the bedroom door open.

Sally lay on our bed, head on my pillow, far away in the land of Nod. Watching us in the garden must have been very tiring so she had come into the house, hooked her nose round the hallway door (as we saw her do after that), then climbed the stairs, pushed the bedroom door open and gone to sleep.

Curiosity was her middle name. When out walking if something caught her eye she would just stop and stare. Her favourite was when she stopped at street corners and learner drivers came reversing round she would just stare through the window at the driver or instructor (she was not fussy which). Anyone arguing or talking loudly was a guaranteed cause for Sal to stop and stare.

34

I can remember having to stop one freezing cold winter's afternoon for Sal to watch two men wiring their outdoor Christmas lights and inflating a six-foot high Father Christmas. Fascinating (for a greyhound, that is). One morning she was in mid-bowel movement when a cat appeared in the drive just off the pavement where she squatted. You could see the look of panic on Sal's face...hang on cat...I'm busy...I'll chase you in a minute....hang on......can't concentrate....blast, he's gone.....

So what do greyhounds eat (apart from cat fur)? In Sal's case, practically anything. Her first night at home with us, Armelle picked up two tangerines and put them on the coffee table as she went to answer the phone. When she came back into the room one of the tangerines was on the table and the other was wandering down the room between Sally's jaws! Sal loved her food, especially fruit. She ate grapes, orange, carrots (raw carrot Sunday morning when prepping dinner was a favourite to crunch in her bed), apple, banana, all human food (especially fond of hot curries, chillies and Italian food) but did not like mushrooms. Sal was generally a quiet girl, and

35

the only time she barked was at five o'clock when it was time for her "dins"! Then she would bark and if this did not initiate a response she would come up and bark directly in your face until you told her grub was on the way. We had not had her long and my mother in law was visiting. It was coming to 5 o'clock and as we sat in the living room we could hear some scuffling from the kitchen. In walked Sal with the empty Frosties box that had been put out in the kitchen bin clasped in her mouth. My mother in law turned to Armelle and said, "I think the dog wants feeding." Sal was a real foodie. It was a rule (and good manners) never to feed her at the kitchen table, but if she was in her bed she would get scraps fed to her so she learned that staying in her bed was a good thing. All food was fine and her system could cope with it very well though there were a few blips, usually with proper dog food. Like one day when my mum was looking after her and she could not find the dog food so she gave her a whole bowl of Winalot dog mixer. Sal had the runs for days. Another time we went to my mum's for Sunday lunch (Sally adored her Nana's Sunday dinners best of all) and the meal was one

36

you did not know whether to eat it or climb it. There was so much mashed potato that when Sal closed her mouth it squirted out of the front between her teeth! Sal never knew when to stop and would eat until she burst. My grandfather had always said that you couldn't overfeed a greyhound; this was proved wrong; the dinner stayed down 5 minutes! She loved gravy dinners, which was something that would come back to haunt us in later life.

Sally was always well-behaved when we took her visiting. We had not had her long when we went to visit Armelle's cousin. As Sal had been so good, he gave us a small piece of cake wrapped in a serviette for her, which she could have later. When we got back to the car, in jumped Sal. As a bit of back story here, this was a new car, a new red 5 door Renault Clio, the first brand-new car I had ever had. Emphasis here, as you can see was on "New". Sal stood on the back seat, head sticking in between the front seats. I gave Sal the small piece of cake which she swallowed in one go, but just before it went down, she did a little cough. Imagine, clean car and dashboard gleaming, and soft, crumbly sponge-cake. There was a fine shower of cake crumbs shot-blasted into the air and across the cab. I swear that I was still finding bits of cake for months after! Sal must have been the biggest mucky pup ever!

Another of her weird habits was her love of fruit juice; one evening I was pouring Armelle a glass of orange juice and I could see Sal was curious, sniffing around. I poured a drop into her bowl and went off to the living room. There was a sound of clanging of dog-collar on tin bowl and in she came. I thought nothing of it until the following night when I poured Armelle a fruit juice and brought it in. Sal followed us in and stood in front of the two of us in front of the glass and barked. And barked. I stood up and went out to the kitchen and she followed me. I opened the fridge door and took out the juice and she licked her lips. I poured her the juice and then went back to the living room. Clang, clang, clang. In came a happy greyhound who then settled on her bed contented. This became a ritual for the rest of her life – if anyone had a fruit juice (pop or wine was not the same and did not have the same effect) then Sal had to have some too.

Somehow she knew things that were bought for her. I'll give two examples; on one occasion we took Sal to a greyhound rescue show and there we bought a bag of dog chocolate drops. She was very well behaved and had never taken chocolates off the table or chairs. We left Sal in the kitchen as we went up to change. When we came down Sal was sitting quietly on her bed beside my chair in the living room. I noticed a plastic bag on the other chair. It was just a clear plastic bag, nothing out of the ordinary. Armelle and I could not remember what the bag was doing there. I picked it up – the bag was empty, no sign of what was in it….except for a small hole in one corner. Sal had seen the bag of chocolates, had carefully pulled a hole in it and eaten the contents without leaving a mess or any evidence and just left the bag where it was on the chair. Well, they were hers anyway.   One Christmas I bought Sal a dog bed and brought it home from work. I put it on the floor in the living room and asked her to sit on it just to see how it fitted – perfectly as it happened. I put the bed back in the black sack it was in and put it behind the chair and out of the way ready to put it away for Christmas. Armelle

and I cooked tea and there was no sign of Sal.
Imagine our amazement when we went back in
the living room and Sal was lying on her new bed.
Not only had she gone behind the chair and
around the cupboard to find the bag, she'd pulled
the bed out and dragged it across the floor and put
it down on top of her other bed. Sal wanted the
bed, knew it was hers, and knew where the bed
should be placed. "Well," said Armelle, "Looks like
she wants her present now and doesn't want to
wait 'til Christmas!".

Winning Ways

Should you have any problems then the Greyhound Rescue group should be there for support. We have only needed them once, when we had to find a kennel at short notice and Gelli Farm came up trumps. We did however like to do our bit to support them. They had regular events a few times a year to keep members up to date and a chance for non-owners to meet dogs as well as allowing Sally to meet old friends. At one show we met her previous owners who had raced her and then passed her to Greyhound Rescue. Sally was originally from Worcestershire but was not much cop as a racer in the major leagues. One day the family from Swansea had a phone call from the dog trainers saying that they had some dogs to get shot of. It was a case of collect them if you want them or else they would not be racing again. The inference was clear.

Sally and her sister were in a shocking state when they were picked up, thin, out of condition and generally in a bad way. They also had a number of wounds. The family fed them up and brought them back into racing trim over the next few months. Sally and her sister Lynsey won a few races in South Wales – they said her racing name was Supersoft. That name really suited her personality. They had taken Sal or her sister into the house occasionally where she had seen the telly for the first time and shown her great interest in it. Perhaps they had not given her the motivation she required – maybe instead of the electric hare there should have been a packet of M&S chilli combo crisps or a mars bar or a TV set for her to follow. After a few more months the family decided that it was time for Sal and her sister to move on. We have all heard the horror stories about greyhounds being drowned, shot, abandoned on the motorway, mutilated (ears cut off so that their identification tattoo cannot be read). This family knew about Greyhound Rescue. They contacted one of the crew and arranged that Sally and her sister would go to a good home – they were very insistent on that. Sally had then come to us and Lynsey had gone to a family in Pembrokeshire. They were very similar to look at but they reckoned that Sal had the nicer personality.

At the Greyhound Rescue Show as I said we met this family. Greyhounds love racing and even enjoy the racing life - what was really telling was the way in which Sally recognised her former owners and how excited and happy she got when she saw them. How she jumped and yapped. If they had mistreated her she would surely never have reacted in that way. They were good people and so very interested in knowing Sally's new owners and how she was adapting to her new life. We learnt a lot about her funny ways and exchanged stories.

As we came into the site we had seen a table with a long queue of people and dogs standing at it. We did not know what was going on but Sal and I joined the queue. It turned out that this was for entering your dog in the show in various categories. We paid our money as a means of supporting the organisation rather than as a serious attempt to win anything. Sally went in for Best Greyhound Bitch and Best Rescued Dog. It was with a lot of excitement that we went into the ring and did our bit. She was pretty well behaved until someone let his or her dogs run off in the background and I suddenly had to cope with a bouncing, yowling coil of noisy excitement that was Sally. I managed to calm her and the judge came over, inspected her and asked us to walk around the circle. I was nervous but Sally was perfectly settled. She walked like she owned the place, head high, stepping like a one of the Welsh cob ponies we had seen at the Royal Welsh Show. As we waited the judge called the dog next to me forward and gave them an award, and then another dog. "Ah well, better luck next time. Not even a third," I told Sally. Then we were called forward. We were not third – she had won best in class. If you want to see a greyhound smile – and they do, a lot! – pin on a rosette. She stood proudly to have her picture taken. Then we left the ring to see my wife.

It was ironic that we had been up against one of the racing dogs now owned by Sally's previous family. My wife laughed – "You won't believe this but when I was standing with the family one of the lady's friends shouted out to us 'Remember that dog you gave away – she just won!'" Armelle said. She did not win anything in the Best Rescue category but we hung on, on what was a very long, hot afternoon for the Best in Show. Sally did not win but she got Best Reserve in show. She was so proud of herself that I thought she was going to burst! And all this with two inches chopped off her tail and the two old wounds on her side!

As she settled she developed more and more of a distinct personality with a more and more wicked sense of humour. When she ran around, chased her toy, or play bowed for you, she smiled and her eyes sparkled. I have a great photo of her jumping around on the lawn; it's not in focus, you

can see she's moving, but she has a huge smile and her eyes are so alive; it's probably the best photo of Sal as it captures the essence of her.

Everyone loved her, from my Mum to the people at the boarding kennels to the people in work with me or my wife who asked for regular updates on what she did next. I also got used to people stopping me in the street and asking about her, whether she was a rescue dog and "Is it true that they make good pets?" When you consider the hard life she had in the big tracks and the way in which she was moved around so much it is amazing that she was such a good natured, well-balanced dog. Sal was an affectionate and loyal gentle giant of a dog with a large character to match. She somehow knew when you were down, and would sit and listen to all your problems without comment or a murmur. She would just sit and listen. When we were on street collections for Greyhound Rescue in all weathers she would allow kids to pat her, poke her and hang from her neck and just soak it all up. She even seemed to know when some people had disabilities and would give them that extra bit of attention or patience.

Sal and my Mum were particularly close. My Mum was in her later 70's when Sal arrived, and her best friend had passed away only a couple of months before. Sal arrived to fill the niche Mam's friend had left. On Tuesday's I would drop Sal off at my Mum's for the day, where she would sit at the foot of the stairs waiting for Mam to get up. They would be inseparable until I collected Sal on the way home from work. If I rang about 4.30 all I would hear in the background was Sal barking – it was nearly tea-time, and Sal had worked out that if you asked Nan for tea earlier it would usually work! On Thursdays Mam would catch the bus up to our house, stopping at the corner shop for a small milky way or Turkish delight bar which was Sal's treat when her Nana arrived. Armelle and I would get home to find Mam sitting watching Countdown with Sal lying in front of her, her head on Mam's leg, looking up at her adoringly. Mam's mobility was gradually decreasing as she got older, but she would insist on having Sal to stay if we went away for a night or so, perhaps to a concert in Bristol. On one occasion we phoned home after the concert for Mam to say that Sal was ok but the snow outside had confused her a bit. What snow? Apparently in the three hours since leaving home there had been an inch of light snow! Mam and her friend

Teresa loved to walk Sal between them and they would take her round the local park. One of the locals said to Mam that the dog was almost as tall as she was! But here's the thing; when someone walked her on the lead she seemed to know to walk to their speed, and she never pulled when my Mum or a child walked her. We all went on a greyhound Rescue street collection in the town centre and when we had finished we had to return badges and literature to another of the team. This meant that both Armelle and I had our arms full and Mam had to walk Sal alongside us. Sal walked gently at my Mum's side, kept looking back at her and shepherded her along until I could come back and collect her.

She was, as we discovered about most greyhounds (or maybe we were very lucky) very affectionate. She liked nothing better than to lie with her head on your foot, or if you sat on the floor with her she would rest her head on your lap. She also liked to lie alongside you on the floor and would roll over so her chest was against yours. I could feel her heart beating against my chest. I read somewhere that someone described their dog (a whippet) as "smelling of warm buttered toast". Again, I know what that means. It is a wonderful feeling to have a being lean against you and just enjoy the comfort of being loved. After a walk, Sal would have a shake and then come back for a cuddle, or if I knelt she would bury her head in my chest and give a huge sigh.

Greyhounds chase small furry things; it's in their nature. Some can be trained to be cat safe, or just are by nature. Sal was not one of those; once on an evening walk she pulled a cat out from under a parked car. She had a mouthful of grey hair as the cat sped down the street unharmed but severely chastened. Sal also had huge claw marks across her face, narrowly missing her eye. Sal never appreciated how dangerous a cat could be! Sally was great with small dogs and seemed to understand the difference between a small dog and a cat or squirrel. The only times she ever snapped at a small dog was when a Westie became too amorous and tried to mount her (she had patiently ignored him for a while but then it got too much) and then when a terrier growled and tried to go for Armelle when she was walking Sal. Fortunately Sal never connected as the terrier would have been mincemeat. She was gentle and

49

patient but would defend her pack if she needed to. Greyhounds are generally not aggressive dogs, their defence is their speed, and they prefer to run away. Only once was Sal attacked by another dog and that was on the cricket pitch behind the house when we walked past a border collie that went for her and tried to bite her through her fleece-lined coat. Sal just looked at that dog with her best greyhound withering stare and walked past. I clipped the collie around the ear.

Prickly Problems

Hedgehogs were Sal's bad habit and I suppose they were her downfall. Sal had learned quite early to ask to go out the garden to the toilet. When she was about ten, one evening she went out in the garden. She was inordinately interested in the bottom corner by the tomato house. When I went out, she was pawing at a hedgehog. I pulled her away and apart from a pricked foot she was ok. For the next few nights I went out before her and looked around in case of any hidden hogs. Nothing. Then a few weeks later she found another and pricked per nose and foot, and her mouth as she tried to pick it up. There can be times when a greyhound can be particularly thick! A few days later she was very sick, so another trip to the vet who suggested the spines had injected muck straight into Sal's bloodstream. Then a month later – it was Guy Fawkes Night – she had a bladder infection and turned the kitchen into Lake Michigan. All I needed was a paddle and a canoe! She even brought a Hedgehog up the garden to me in her mouth, looking ever so pleased. She could not understand why I scolded her and took it off her (!). These infections were a precursor to more serious conditions.

As mentioned previously, Sal never chewed any of her food and she had frequent bouts of very loose poo and upset stomachs as she grew older. When she was young, her digestive system could cope but as she got older it was not so easy. One particular day she was just not right, was off her food (not like her at all) and so I took her to the vets (visiting our parking space again). She began over salivating, and coughing. Armelle had decided to stay behind to prepare tea. I took Sally in and the vet gave her a thorough examination and pronounced Sal had pancreatitis and should go to the main surgery. OK, I asked, should I make an appointment for any particular time the next day? No, he said, take her down now, he was ringing ahead, and yes, it was life threatening. I was shell-shocked. I drove as fast as was (fairly legally) possible to the main surgery and took Sal in and she was taken to a crate. I was told again that she was a very sick dog.

Sal hovered at death's door for a few days and had some VERY expensive treatment. She was on a drip for two days, and over the week lost two kilos in weight. We rang three or four times each day to see how she was doing. On the fourth day I went to collect Sal and had to practically carry her out to the car. She was over the worst but looked so thin and shaky on her feet. She was really spaced out. She did not eat and hardly drank for another two days but gradually her appetite came back... She was on plain rice and fish for a week but then we slowly brought her back to a normal diet. However, her diet would never be the same again. Basically the gravy and rich food had gradually knackered her system so from then on we had to monitor fat and protein levels in her food. Sal pulled through this and lived for another few years enjoying a semi-healthier lifestyle and diet.

Sal was very laid back and pretty much took life as it came. She coped with any disruptions to her daily pattern with barely a shrug. In 2006 we decided to extend the house. This meant the drive would be dug up, the garden dug up, kitchen roof taken off, and the upstairs knocked about – a lot of noise, mess and chaos. We stayed in the house during all the building work. As the builders arrived, Sal would just sit in her bed in the kitchen and watch them pass. Lunchtimes and tea-breaks were great as she would help the builders eat their food. She was so quiet that one morning they even thought she was dead! She was interested in what they were doing, and every night when we got home from work and after spending an hour or so dusting and cleaning Sal would insist on having a tour to see what had changed. After the scaffolding went up I had to shin up a ladder most nights to realign the satellite dish which the builders had taken down and so was temporarily propped on a sloping roof with bricks. Sal would stand below and watch me through the gaps in the scaffolding planks. The best story of the builders was where one day two of them were arguing. I was coming through the (what would become) workshop and one of the builders asked me, "Is your dog's name Sausage?" No, I said, it's Sally. "There you are" he said to his mate, "Told you." I pointed out that I did call her Sally Sausage as a nick-name so in fact they were both right. Outside what became the new back door was a new manhole but until it was finished there was no inspection cover, just a piece of thick sterling board. As I let Sal out one evening the board had moved and she screamed as her front legs slipped into the hole. As I grabbed her; the neighbour's back door flew open to see what had happened to Sal. She was shaking a bit but ok, the only damage being two fine lines on the front of her shins where the brick had shaved off the short hair. Building work, it must be noted, never disrupted Sal's weekly trips to her Nana, and in fact for a few days a week she would go there if the work was particularly noisy/dirty or there was the need to have doors left wide open. For a few weeks she even had to have her bed moved to the living room, and for two days (the only time during the entire build) we all decamped to my mother's. It took over six months but then the building work was over, and the garden was reset and the new lawn laid, all ready for Sal to lie on in the summer. Despite a sudden fall of snow in April, we had a few nice days in early May and Sal decided that the new patio was very good and pronounced it just right to lie on and catch a few rays.

We had not really noticed that our Sal was getting older. She was a white and fawn dog, and the years never really showed on her face. Looking back, in the photos her fawn was getting a bit lighter, and we noticed that when we went for walks she started to want to sit down for a bit of a rest. This was especially so on the beach, where she discovered warm sand. She had always loved going to Oxwich beach and sitting in the sand and was reluctant to go back to the car. Quite often it would look awful as I would have to tow a recalcitrant greyhound over the sand like a canine plough! Over the last few years she grew to love the soft warm sand even more and would insist on lying in the sun-warmed patches on the walk back to the car. We took her to the National Museum of Wales at St. Fagan's and even here she enjoyed people stopping to make a fuss of her as she took time out for a break on her tour of the park.

One evening before her tea Armelle took Sally over the cricket pitch. She was walking slowly, but still game for a walk. Armelle noticed that she was a bit quieter than usual, and at one point Sal sat down on the pitch in the sun for a rest but seemed otherwise to be ok. When they got back I had come home from work and we made and ate our tea together. Something was not quite right with Sal though we could not put our fingers on it... After tea Sal started panting heavily and she was sick. She sat on the sheepskin rug by her Nana's chair and was getting worse, crying a little and looking a bit distressed. We rang the vets (practically now on speed dial) and I had to carry her out to the car as her legs had gone. At the vets they met me and carried Sal into the examination room. They took a set of bloods, and checked her heart and her lips and tongue colour – too pale for my liking. Sal seemed to come too in the exam room and I will never forget how she sat up and looked around the room at each of us in turn, seeming to sum each of us up, satisfying herself that we were there for her. The vet suggested she had a stomach infection and we should take her home, he gave her a painkilling jab, she would be fine by the morning. I carried her to and from the car and put her in her bed at home. At one stage she tried to get up but I asked to sit back in her bed. She curled up and started to drift into sleep, occasionally opening her eyes to see if I was there. I sat on the kitchen chair next to her as the evening drew into morning but about 2 o'clock, as

I could see she was sleeping and still hear her breathing, I moved to the chair in the lounge nearest the kitchen door so I could watch over her. When I awoke at 6 o'clock I saw she was still. On checking her I found that she had passed away gently in her sleep. Clumsy, awkward, accident prone but lovely gentle Sal had slipped away. The vet had realised she had had a heart attack; there was nothing that could be done and had not wanted her to die in the surgery alone but at home. I will always be grateful for that. I rang the vets to let them know, and arranged to take her down for her to be cremated.

Removal was a less dignified matter. Weighing 27 kilos and being a real dead weight I could not lift her. Armelle and I wrapped her in her duvet and holding two corners each we struggled to carry her across the living room to the front door. Unfortunately for Sal her head popped out at one stage and I banged her against the settee and another time we dropped her on the floor. I could almost hear her tut-tutting as she looked down from above. Sorry Sally love.

Two weeks later I collected a lovely wooden casket with her name engraved on a little brass plaque. Sal was laid to rest on the edge of the lawn she loved so much, near where she hunted hedgehogs, under a flowering currant which is forever known as Sally's tree. We think of her always.

Fostering?

After Sal I was lost and Armelle and I fell between leaving a long time to grieve or rushing into getting another dog. I was keen to get another dog quickly, not because I wanted to replace Sal but to have someone else to nurture. Armelle on the other hand was reluctant to rush into anything. So, in a sort of compromise, we ended up fostering. Fostering is a skill; it takes patience, it takes an ability to understand how dogs think and react, to see things how they do, and it takes a fair amount of love. More importantly the fosterer has to assess a dog's problems, see what the dog needs and then know when to pass the dog on to a home or another fosterer. Parting with a dog is really hard; you don't want to admit defeat as it makes you feel that you've let the dog down, and you will inevitably have bonded with the dog no matter what. I can best explain by talking about our first foster, a greyhound called Queenie.

We contacted a local rescue centre about rehoming a greyhound and whether any likely dogs were available. There was a dog that had been brought in and needed a home. She was quiet and non-destructive. We collected this squat but pretty white and black greyhound bitch whose background was a bit sketchy. She was great when she came home, took to the garden without a hitch. She followed us around downstairs, did not jump on the furniture or worktops, and was pretty laid back. She did not like a high sided bed but preferred a duvet folded on the floor. The first night was fine; she was quiet and clean.

Things boded well. She was a great traveller and loved trips in the car. We began to try her for longer and longer periods during the day at home and she was fine. However, after the first week of quiet nights we began to see that Queenie had her issues. She was clawing and banging the kitchen door in the middle of the night; I went down and tried to get her to go out in case she needed a toilet break. She settled in her bed and I returned to my bed. Over the week the banging and clawing got worse, always starting about 3 o'clock in the morning. I began to leave the living room door open, in case it was the kitchen that she didn't like. We even had a night-light so that the room was not so dark. This worked for a while as then she would sleep on the living room floor. She really did not like the ceramic tiles on the kitchen floor. Instead Queenie began clawing the carpet and messing in the living room. Every night Armelle would be woken up by me Vaxing the carpet about 3 o'clock in the morning. It got so that I was not sleeping at night, I would lie in bed waiting for Queenie's clawing. For some reason she would never mess on the tiled floor but only on carpet. Maybe, we began to wonder, it was difficult for her to squat on the smooth floor, or maybe the carpet reminded her of grass? Her toileting habits were very strange; she would go first thing in the morning and then despite being put out she would hold for hours. It was a month before she started to toilet on her walks and she did not seem to mark. This we put down to a lack of confidence which we felt sure would develop as she got more settled.

We began to think it odd that she never attempted the stairs and was not very good on steps, which we thought was because she had never really seen them before. She was usually good with other dogs and with people and children, though she was twitchy when dogs went behind her, especially male dogs. I took her into shops with me and she was very well behaved, would stand and wait by my side, and was content to be fussed. Somehow though, I felt she did not have the eagerness to be fussed that Sally had, but maybe with was because she was still not long off the track.

The strangest thing about Queenie was her fascination with speedboats! One really lovely summer afternoon we took her down to Mumbles and we walked along the promenade. Suddenly she stopped, totally rigid, eyes out on stalks. She was transfixed, watching a water-skier going past, towed by a speedboat. She pulled Armelle and I along the prom and down the slipway where she stood on the edge of the water, feet in the lapping waves, watching. It was the first time I had really seen her eyes sparkle. We stood there for ages as she watched the boats go past, looking left and right like the spectators at Wimbledon.

We would sometimes find Queenie standing in the living room staring into space and her nose running. We were used to Sal's nose running when she was happy but it did not seem to be the same with Queenie. We contacted the rescue centre to give them an update and feedback and we gathered a bit more information about Queenie that had come from the fosterer who had rescued her. It turned out that she was a good racer who had run 250 races over three years and she was over 6 years old. I began to wonder whether she was unable to do steps, difficulty squatting, occasionally looking in pain – did she have some underlying medical problem maybe? We took her to our vet who x-rayed her and diagnosed arthritis in her hips; she had been over-raced and was in pain because her hip-joints were worn-out. We started her on painkillers which seemed to help and then we even contacted an animal behaviourist to see whether we could break her out of the overnight cycle of messing.

By this stage I was exhausted as I had had disturbed sleep for 3 months. We began to think that maybe Queenie was beyond us and reluctantly we spoke to the rescue centre and arranged for Queenie to go back. I cried as we handed her over in the car park and though I knew it was right I broke my heart. I was upset because I felt we had let her down.

We were contacted by the fosterer who had originally rescued Queenie. She had been sold from a Midlands track to a man in Cardiff who kept her in a shed with two male dogs. They had not been neutered and Queenie had never been spayed. Queenie would not mate with them and she refused to race so he would not feed her. It appeared that she had been on the receiving end of some beatings too. We realised then where a lot of her demons came from;

- Fear of the dark – the dark shed with the other dogs
- Did not like male dogs sniffing round her
- Held for hours as she was only toileted first thing in the morning (when let out of the shed) and then early evening (when the guy came home from work).
- Would not mess on a hard surface as she was beaten if she messed on the shed floor
- Raced to destruction

Queenie's was not an entirely sad story; she became a permanent foster as she was never really able to go to a normal home. Sponsored by a greyhound charity, she went to a house with a large garden where she could wander in and out at will and live a quiet life. Also, our experience with Queenie though distressing at the time showed us that we had the patience to foster, and with our experience of greyhounds we could help to see what made that particular dog tick, and what they needed. I had amazed myself at my patience and that I had in all the mess and frustration never lost my temper or even raised my voice at Queenie. On her part, she had never growled or snapped. None of this was her fault; it was all because of what people had done to her.

In Walked Sam

It was a few months later that we had a call
from the rescue centre; they had a dog that
needed a foster home. So, over Armelle and I
went. We sat in the kitchen as this dog was
fetched in; she was a small black greyhound who
came over to us for a fuss but then wandered off
and then back, all the while talking away to herself
in small yaps and whines. Black dogs, we found
out later, were really difficult top home as people
don't think that they are pretty. How could anyone
think that – this particular little girl had the prettiest
sparkling deep brown eyes, so deep you could
practically swim in them!. She really was a tiny
thing though, about two-thirds Sal's size. This
little girl's racing name was Wagga Nell so we
could either call her Nellie or something sounding
like Wagga. I was adamant I was not shouting
Nellie on the cricket pitch, so the little noisy one
was christened Sammy. We put her into Sally's
old martingale collar (the one her Nan had one
year bought her for her birthday) and took her out

to the car. In she jumped - things were looking pretty positive.

When we got Sam out she was sick from head to tail. Oh dear, this was not a good start, it appeared Sammy was not a good traveller! She hopped out of the hatchback and went straight in, through the house and out the back for a sniff and a pee. She trotted back into the kitchen, took a look at her bed and settled in it for a sleep. Her first walk was great, and it was nice to meet people again. You never realise how many people you get to know (and they you) when walking a dog - we saw friends we had not seen in months.

The next day was a greyhound rescue street collection, so Sam and I were off to the city centre. Unfortunately the traffic was heavy due to a local soccer derby and by the time we got to the car park in town Sam had thrown up again. I cleaned her up and despite everything, she was happy to stand around, meet people and do her bit. She wore Sal's collar and her red waterproof coat (which was far too big for her) but she looked wonderful. She was great with children but not so good with dogs; she was a little bit shy. She threw up again in the car on the way back but when we got home she slept all afternoon.

We did not consider that the car sickness was an issue for us as she was a foster and would not be with us permanently. It would be someone else's problem - Sam would be a house-dog unless someone could find the right medication. We could not get her into the local village without her dribbling and drooling. Maybe it was psychological – we would have to try building up her time in the car, and make it nice trips so the experience was positive.

So, the next week instead of walking Sam up to the local park we put her in the hatchback. When we got there I went round to open the hatch – and out jumped Sam and off she ran! Flip! She flew straight past Armelle and I, past the parked cars and down past the tennis courts. We were terrified she would run out onto the main road but instead she ran the other way into the park. After 10 minutes we cornered her near the tennis courts and I clipped her lead on. Phew! Armelle said to me as we walked back to the car "I was beginning to wonder how we'd tell the Rescue Kennels we lost their dog!" We learnt from that day to clip

71

Sam to a lead inside the car, and then switch to a walking lead after we had opened the boot, so that she could not get out.

Off to the vets; we tried some tablets based on milk which would relax her. It worked to an extent; Sam would throw up but was very chilled about it. "Hey, let's go for a trip in the car....I'll be sick but what the heck....I get a nice walk at the end of it." It worked for a while but still did not get over the throwing up. She would never get the same experiences of Sal or even Queenie as she was not going to be able to do longer journeys.

A month after Sam arrived was Christmas and she had presents and her own Xmas lunch. Sam was another foodie, she enjoyed her food no end. Unlike Sally though, Sam knew when she was full. She would eat and stop when full, and rarely went back to any food she had left. She loved all cooked food, all cooked vegetables but could not understand what raw vegetables were about. Whereas Sal would be excited by a raw carrot, Sam would look at you as if you were a Martian. "What, you want me to cook it myself?" Curries, chillies, everything was great. Fruit juice was a no-no. And she chewed. Whereas Sally had bad breath and teeth that needed brushing, Sammy had great teeth. Everything was chewed and crunched. Sam really was a little princess. She was good with small dogs, and would wag her tail at cats. She did not have an aggressive bone in her body. No wonder she was not very good on the track.

We found out that our Sam was an Irish girl who had had 2 trials and a race at the track at Youghal but was not very good. She ended up in a van full of Irish dogs at the local track in South Wales where she had been taken on by a trainer who was prone to giving her a thumping. We knew the kennel maids who had looked after the dogs (members of our rescue charity) and they recognised Sam, and she had recognised them, especially when one of them gave her a digestive biscuit. Sam had usually been bullied by the other dogs and would huddle at the back of the kennel but she would come forward when the girls handed out the digestive biscuits as a treat. Sam never forgot the biscuits or them. It was lovely to think that despite the cruelty in her early life, at least someone had shown our little princess some kindness.

We were very strict with Sam and her housetraining went really well. She was always very well behaved and never begged and was never a thief. Like Sal, I would put her food out and she would wait (quivering usually) to be told she could eat. When we ate she sat in her bed and waited. She did learn though that Nana was a soft touch. My Mum came to live with us after the onset of her Alzheimer's, and Sam knew that Nana always had a biscuit after her meal. So, as soon as the table was cleared, she would be up and standing next to my Mum, waiting for a piece of biscuit! It was her only bad habit though. Apart from the time we went to a greyhound charity jumble sale where she was allowed to wander amongst the people. I had just remarked that, like Sally, she was really well behaved. As I finished speaking Sam picked up a Viennese whirl off the table and walked off, crunching as she went.

She was generally very well behaved but in the early months as she settled she pushed the boundaries a fair bit. We had to remember that after all she had never been in a house before.

74

She was typically inquisitive and wanted to know what you were doing, so if I was fiddling putting up a shelf, she would come and see and then wander off. Whereas Sal would stay by my side to "help", Sam would get bored and wander back to a comfy spot for a sleep. The back bedroom had always been a bit of a tip but we decided it was time for a refurbishment. The drill came out to fit some shelves along with tins of paint and brushes for the skirting boards. I was working with the drill, marking up and setting it all out and then drilling. As I was working Sam stuck her head around the door just to see what was going on. Nothing caught her interest so she wandered off to the front bedroom to the Big Bed. I took the drill apart and put the chuck key and drills on the floor as I went to the bathroom to wash my hands. I came back passing Sam on the landing on her way back to the bedroom. Where was she off to? I followed her into our room and I could see she was carrying something - what did she have in her mouth? Would you believe it was a chuck key and four three inch chipboard screws. She was quite content to let me take them out of her mouth – she was very lucky not to have swallowed one of the screws! The next day I was painting the skirting board and Sam was (presumably) asleep on the bed in the front bedroom. Once again I went to wash my hands, and Armelle came upstairs to talk to me. I heard a noise in the other room but thought nothing more of it. I walked past the back bedroom where I had been working and there was no-one in there so I continued into the front bedroom. There was Sam, sitting in the middle of the bed, pleased as punch with a 2" paintbrush full of white paint clamped between her jaws. "Look at me, I'm helping!" I extracted the brush before she managed to paint the duvet cover.

Another morning – and it was a cold winter's morning – Sam had gone out to the garden and after twenty minutes I heard a loud noise and Sam came running up the garden, passing Armelle on the garden path. She trotted by me in the kitchen and went into the living room. There was a puddle of water on the floor…in fact, there was a trail if water across the kitchen and out the back door. I followed the trail towards the fishpond, where the concrete ornaments had been pushed off the side. "I've found what the noise was," I called to Armelle. Sam had been climbing up on the side of the pond and had slipped into the water, knocking the stone kingfisher and owl that stood sentry on the edge of the murky water in with a thud and a splash. Startled, Sam had clambered out of the pond and had run back into the house, taking muddy pond water with her! Sam was soaking and was standing in the living room in front of the gas fire, steaming, clumps of duckweed on her coat and her nose! That was the last time she did that!

As the months went by, it became obvious that this little foster had no intention of moving on and we had no intention of parting with her. Whereas Sal had gone everywhere with us, Sam was content to spend time at home. The deal was that when we were home then the three of us would be together.

Armelle finished work the year that Sal died and so was usually at home with Sam. Sam was always talkative, and would answer if asked whether she wanted something "Yuss". She learnt that if she stood by the living room door when Armelle was busy and she cried then she began to be let upstairs. Like Sal, she loved the "Big Bed".

If we had been out for the evening, or if the weather was bad and she could not go out, or if she was just whingey, just ask Sam if she wanted the "Big Bed" – she was by the door like a shot. Again like Sal, she loved to lie between us, on her back. Unlike Sal, who used to lie at the foot of the bed with her feet in the air, Sam was more sensible and kept away from the edge of the bed (I remember Sally once sliding off the bed onto her back and almost getting wedged between the bed and the chest of drawers).

Lying in bed one Sunday morning with the papers I looked at the mug I had bought a few years before just after Sal had died; it was a couple in bed with a little black greyhound in between them, on its back, one leg in the air, and the legend on it read "When its good to be the third person in a marriage". As I read it, the little black greyhound between us shifted to make herself more comfortable and pushed a cheesy front foot into my face.

The only thing with letting Sam on the bed in the evening was that it was a problem to get her to go back downstairs; not that she ever cried or scraped the kitchen door for she was grateful for a soft bed, safety and affection, it was just that she was reluctant to leave. We developed a routine that I would go downstairs and cut off a small piece of cheese. By the time I had closed the fridge door she would be thundering through the living room for her cheese. This was intended to be a temporary routine until she realised that when I went downstairs it would be good for her to follow me.

The White Dog

Armelle and I had often spoken about the "White Dog" keeping an eye on us and sometimes I could feel that Sal was there just out of the corner of my eye. This I put down to me being daft. However, there were a couple of strange things that made me wonder if that was not me being daft. We began to notice that sometimes Sam would sit or stand and just appear to be looking and listening to someone or something. Not staring into the distance, or watching the wall but looking just above her height and just in front of her. It was as if she was listening to someone talking to her and she was often quite intent. I thought it was just me at first until Armelle also commented on it. We became to joke that she was getting a debrief from the White Dog who was watching over us. The other strange event was in our local park. Sam loved watching squirrels and loved to chase them to the length of her lead or I would run with her so she could chase them up a tree. If I said, "Squirrel" Sam's ears would prick up, her eyes open wide and she would stiffen with

81

excitement. One summer was a really poor one for squirrels; whenever we were in the park we rarely saw them and it was a great disappointment to our little black trainee squirrel-hound.   This particular day, Armelle and I were coming back through the park and as usual there had not been a squirrel in sight. I happened to say out loud, "Come on Sal, let's give Sammy a squirrel to chase, please?" and almost immediately a squirrel popped out from the hedge about ten feet ahead. We duly chased it to the other hedge where it ran up a tree! I have never doubted since that we are indeed watched over by four-footed angels; if anything, this has been a comfort to us to think they are always with us.

Sam was a very gentle soul; she wagged her tail at cats and only ever made half-hearted attempt to chase them. She did once see Fluffy's tail sticking out under the gate and tried to grab it (Fluffy was an elderly Persian cross moggie who lived up the street and had outlived Sal). She chased squirrels but never really tried to catch them, she just loved the chase. It was the same when we met rabbits (of more, later). One summers evening we let Sam out and off she went down the garden. She came back and barked at me (she rarely barked). It was a classic "Lassie" moment where she wanted us to follow her. She led us down the garden to the corner by the tomato house, where there was a small hedgehog. Once she had shown us, Sam went back into the house. This became a regular thing when the hogs were around, we had to go and see her little friends. Whereas Sal saw them as playthings, Sam saw them as visiting friends.

Sam's sensitivity was something quite amazing; our next door neighbour, Betty, had been very close to our Sally, who would stand by the fence waiting for Betty to come out to give her a biscuit.

Betty had been upset when Sal had died but was very pleased to see little Sam arrive. Not long after Sam came to us, Betty was diagnosed with terminal cancer. Whenever Betty came into our house, Sam would sit at her feet and look up at her., watching her intently. Whenever Sam went for a walk, she began to stop outside Betty's gate and Armelle would have to take her in to see Betty. As her illness progressed, Sam became more and more reluctant to leave Betty's side when we went to come home. They seemed to need one another, and they spent a lot of time together during her illness. On one occasion, just before we were due to go on vacation, Sam was particularly reluctant to go, and she even sat in the hallway to prevent Armelle opening the door to leave Betty's house. She was insistent on staying so Armelle had to wait with her for a while longer before Sam agreed to leave. "You know I won't see you again, Sammy" Betty told her. It was true; when we cam back from holidays we heard that Betty had passed away. For months afterwards, Sam would stop at the end of Betty's garden path and look at the house but would not try and go through the gate. It was as if she was remembering something but knew that Betty was not at home anymore.

We began to see Sam's car-sickness as a potential problem now as we really wanted to get her to come out with us. When we first had her she could not travel a mile without frothing and dribbling. It got so that we could do a couple of miles but even this was a bit hit or miss. Usually as we turned into our road I would look in the reversing mirror and see her shoulders going as she threw up in her bed in the hatchback. We started carrying up a clean-up kit of kitchen roll, poop scoop bags (great for scraping up sick!) and moist cleanup wipes. We tried different travel-sickness tablets for children or animals – after checking that they were safe for greyhounds – but nothing really worked. Some made her relaxed so she threw-up but did not care and others made her drowsy and sick. Someone mentioned to me a homeopathic remedy based on cockleshells (cocculus) which was supposed to suppress the gag reflex. This worked quite well so we could go a couple of miles which meant that trips to Uncle Gareth and Auntie Nesta became viable, and trips to Morriston Park. This was great. Change of scenery, trip in the car, meeting people. However, long journeys were still not possible as the motion was too much. Finally another friend saw an advert in their vets for tablets called Cerenia. We asked our vet; they were quite new, could only be used for 2 consecutive days but lasted 24 hours (so ideal for weekends). They were also £7 each! Armelle and I agreed that if it meant Sam could come out with us and see the beaches and woods, then we'd give it a go. So, the first trip was down to Mumbles, through the thick Swansea traffic, an ideal test. The last time we had gone there the shoulders went just as we got into the car park. This time she was ok. We had a lovely walk in the sunshine and even shared a bag of chips in the back of the car and Sam was not sick at all. From then on we could go to Dinefwr Park, or Gnoll Park, or Three Cliffs Bay. On one occasion she was sick on the way, but fine for the rest of the trip. On short trips we used cocculus but for longer ones we used Cerenia.

Our gentle little girl was a real wuss when it came to having her claws clipped (Sal was nearly the same but not as bad as Sam). We took her to the Vets one day and the vet cut one front

claw but just caught the quick and the scream
Sam issued was absolutely incredible, truly blood-
curdling. He tried another foot but it was no good,
we had to call it a day. She got herself so wound
up that the blood was pumping out of the cut claw.
We went out into the waiting room and the five
people out there were white with fear. I smiled
nervously and told them it was ok, she was only
having her claws trimmed. She was happy to
have a fuss then, even with the Vet, but she was
in no way going to have her claws done. I bought
a clipper and even tried to cut them myself but she
was still not happy about it. She would not bite
me or snap, she would just pull her foot away from
me. I then bought a diamond-edged nail file and
reluctantly she would allow Armelle or me to file
her nails. Another friend had a Malamute that did
not like having his claws done so he went to a
local pet store that had a grooming parlour
attached. Here they put him into a hoist that lifted
him off the floor and he was unable to resist.
Willing to try anything we took Sam down, handed
them the lead and said we would be back in ten
minutes. We were convinced part of the reason
she cried out was that she sensed we were

87

nervous so we gave the shop a wide berth. When we went back, Sam was fine and Helen the groomer said she had not been any bother. Helen had also had a black greyhound and was keen to hear Sam's story. She looked forward to meeting Sammy again. Off Sam went, back in the car but we got stuck in traffic on the way home and, despite the cocculus, she was sick again!

Sam and The Van

Armelle's Mum died and she was also
made redundant so we had an unfortunate sum of
money. Part of it, Armelle decided, she would like
to spend on a motorhome; it was the sort of
frivolous spend that her mother would approve of.
That was how we ended up with an Autoquest 140
parked in our drive. We had read that some
carsick dogs were better in big vehicles so odds
on that Sam would be better in the motorhome.

We started to get Sam used to the van by
just opening the side door, letting her in and then
sitting on the lounge seating with her. Sam loved
to sit and watch out the window at people passing
by. Then we took her in the van to a local country
park about 10 miles away. She was ok but we
had to watch the speed we travelled at as going
too fast round the lanes was not good for her.
She was definitely better in the van, sitting just
behind our driving seats in the walkway beside the
side door, on some towels in case of any
unexpected throwing up. We tried her on the
cocculus and found that she could travel a bit

further; we took her down to Three Cliffs in the van and she was great. The trip home was a bit much though; we pulled up outside the house and Sam was looking the worse for wear. We opened the door just as a family was walking past and their 6 year old daughter was saying to her Mum, "Oh look, what a lovely doggie," as Sam leaned out, eyes wide and dry retching. Fortunately she kept her dinner down until an hour later when the living room carpet had it. She loved going in the van - she would even stop outside the door when we walked her past on her daily walks.

One trip we took that Sam really seemed to enjoy was Dinefwr Park near Llandeilo. This was a National Trust property with a car park that suited a motorhome a treat; a lovely spot at the bottom of the car park, with the old fish-pond behind, the old Castle and castle woods to our right. The best thing was that each direction you headed there was a different walk, whether it was woodland, or water meadow, or pasture. There were ducks and geese, white park cattle, rabbits, squirrels and deer. And people and other dogs. Sam was always shy of other dogs but here meeting dogs on a walk was not so frightening, though I'm not sure why. Sam loved it there. On one trip she was bursting for a wee as we came up the drive and parked up. I put her lead on and opened the door and she leapt out and we hastily found a patch of grass for her to empty her bladder. I turned round and tried to take her back to the van for me to change my shoes and put a jacket on but no chance; Sam wanted to have her walk, and only a pee would not do at all, she was not going to be short-changed! It was a real job to get her to jump in but we were straight out and she got her exercise. Then back to the van for a cup of tea and some cake or a sandwich (with fresh tongue just bought that morning from the farm shop), share the sandwiches round between the three of us, and off on another walk. She was particularly keen on Castle Woods, snuffling in amongst the bluebells when they were in season). Sam was even brave enough to walk up the steps of the castle onto the parapet with the incredible view down the Tywi valley towards Dryslwyn. These trips required a Cerenia as it was that bit too far for cocculus and she was absolutely tremendous on them.

91

Feeling brave, we planned our first family trip for the three of us in the van. It was a few weeks before Armelle and I were taking the van to France so it was a chance to shake-down any issues. The weather was predicted to be reasonable; we booked a night on a certified location (licensed for 5 vans and no more) in the Tywi Valley, then two nights at Abermarlais, near Llandovery. It all started really well as the CL was lovely, in a meadow not far from Dryslwyn Castle. We did have en encounter with a snooty caravan owner who approached me when I was just lining the van up to point out that I had to be 6 meters away from him for safety reasons. I nodded and waved, whilst Armelle muttered about him being a pratt and that we had not even parked up at that stage. All sorted, Sam and I went for a wee. The field we were on had been cut that morning, and it had also rained so we both carried in big clods of grass on our feet. I wiped Sammy's feet and took off my shoes and stood in a puddle. Sammy! I figured that she had had an accident, which was not like her at all. I dabbed the carpet with kitchen roll and noticed the water smelt bleachy. Definitely not wee. I checked again – there was water leaking from under the heater unit, which proved to be from the washroom water pipe. So, we could not use the on board water tanks. Not a problem, we would use the gallon water containers and when we needed to wash, use kettles and jugs. We had a great night, had a lovely walk around the village and all slept well. We pulled out the double bed, threw the duvet on and jumped in and Sam followed. She slept at the foot of the bed in between us. I was awakened about seven o'clock the next morning by a black greyhound standing in between us wagging her tail and grinning like an idiot!

That day we spent the morning and had lunch at Dinefwr and then wended our way towards Llandovery and Abermarlais. It was a small site, a little dated but for all that it was quaint and very clean and the staff were brilliant. We had a good explore, Armelle and Sam did the wall of death along the river bank, threatening to fall in, and we sat down to a lovely tea back at the van. By nine o'clock we were all shattered so settled down to sleep. After a couple of hours, I woke as the van was moving and Sam was crying. I asked her what the matter was. She looked at me and cried. She was shaking terribly, like one of those roadside pneumatic drills. She stood up and wagged her tail and tip-toed across the bed. She did not seem in any pain, and though shaking, was not distressed – her eyes were wide and sparkling. OK, must be toilet time. I put on some clothes, got my torch and we opened the door. It was amazing; in the space of thirty yards we saw about a dozen or more rabbits! Sam was so excited but just like the hedgehogs, she had no kill instinct, she just wanted to chase them and run back to me. She did manage a toilet stop but all she really wanted to do was jump with the rabbits. It reminded me of the Peanuts cartoon with Snoopy as the Easter Beagle dancing with the Easter bunnies. Three times that night we were woken by the bed shaking like an earthquake – an incredibly over-excited greyhound could hear and smell rabbits and it was too much for her little head. By seven o'clock when it was time to get up properly, Sammy was shattered. She could hardly put one foot in front of the other as I climbed down the step to take her for her first short walk. Around one corner we saw some rabbits again and she skipped to the end of her extendable lead and then ran back to me. "Look Dad, Rabbits!" We had the same performance the next night with our vibrating greyhound shaking the whole van, despite Armelle and I her telling her to stop it and settle down. When we got home after lunch on the Monday we were all very relaxed though a bit the worse for wear sleep-wise. Sam slept for most of that day and the next but unfortunately we could not as I had to go back to work!

Sam really was a different character to Sal in so many ways. Sam was quiet and not boisterous at all, slight of build, and happy to sit on the bed, or lie on the couch in the van and watch the world go by. She never had Sal's confidence with the world and her demons were things that were strange, or rather strangely familiar. As an example of what I mean, one day we took Sam to Crawley Woods on the Gower. We crossed the busy main road – no problem – and came down through the field towards the woods, which ran down to Oxwich beach below. In the middle of the hedge at the end of the field there was a stile. This was difficult as Sam had not learned to jump over a stile or climb over it, but it was manageable. However, this was not ordinary stile,

95

but one where you pulled up the central post to let the dog through. Sam was a bit reluctant to go though on the way down but on the way back up it was a different matter. Imagine from her perspective; all she could see was a wooden frame with a central wooden bar that lifted and she had to be pushed through. To her, it was being put into a travel crate or worse, it was like the Trap at the track. The only way to get her back was for me to lift her over the stile which was not easy. Little things like this which were not an issue to Sal was difficult and scary to Sam. Just like Sal, she was very affectionate and very caring. She would sit in the evenings on the living room floor at home, usually in between the two of us, or if my mum was there, on the floor in the centre, watching my mother intently. It was as if she knew she was not quite right and needed protecting. Sam even had a kind-of worried look of concentration on her brow as she watched over her Nana. Sam realised that her Nan liked to have toast for breakfast. Now Sam had developed a real love of toast, hot or cold, but preferably with butter on it.   She developed a real bond with my Mum, not the same as with Sal but still very close. Armelle would bring down Mam's toast crusts each morning and put them in Sam's bowl. The first thing Sam would do was take out a crust, go into the living room and place it on the rug in front of my mother's chair (my mother would invariably still be in bed at this time). She would then go back and eat the rest of the crusts. It was as if she knew that they were Nan's crusts and Nana had to have a share too.

As Mam was getting less and less mobile, we began to take her with us to Gnoll Park or Dinefwr; the whole pack together, which seemed to please Sammy immensely. Armelle would walk ahead with Sam on her lead, and I would follow on with Mam in her wheelchair. Sam would stop every few yards to check we were all still following. Back in the van she would assume her position sprawled out at the end of one of the bench seats, head on a cushion and dozing. She would sit up when the food was about but then, back to sleep again. If we were at Dinefwr Mam would sit in the van with a cup of tea whilst we took the hound up to the Castle and back. Either way, both Mam and Sam had a great time! Where Sally had come along at the right time after Mam's

97

best friend had died, the van had arrived at the time when it made taking her out much easier and more rewarding.

As the Van was less of an issue for travel sickness we would even use it to take Sam down to see Maggie in the groomers and have her claws clipped. It seemed to work except again for the times we were stuck in Swansea traffic and a very queasy dog came out at the home end of the journey.

The best holiday we ever had was in Pembrokeshire as a mid-August break. We stayed on a five-van Farm site near Wolfscastle, where Armelle had family. We had loads of places to walk up the quiet lanes, Sam saw chickens and she even heard the rabbits again (though this time she did not vibrate all night!). We drove into St. David's one day and went round the Cathedral Close. Sam did disgrace herself by peeing in the river by the Bishop's Palace as people were looking on. We sat on the grass outside the door under the shelter of a tree whilst Armelle looked around the Cathedral, and I took a few photos of Sammy. I could hear people saying how beautiful she was, and one tourist remarking that she must be having her portrait taken. Another afternoon we went round Scolton Manor Country Park where Sam encountered pigs for the first time. She was not too sure of them as they were big, smelled funny and had teeth.

We ended that afternoon buying fish and chips from the award-winning chip-shop in Letterston.

Sam sprawled on her couch and slept the sleep of the just. That Sunday we visited Armelle's Auntie who was 97. Sam was invited in too and she was very well behaved and this time did not disgrace the family name. It was a smashing holiday.

In a Class of Her Own

Sam was not good with other dogs; she had been bullied by the others at the kennels (we knew that from what Pauline and Olwen the kennel-maids had told us). Small barking dogs frightened her, and on two occasions large dogs had come over to her in the park and tried to mount her. One had been a Rhodesian ridgeback and we were very glad when the owner eventually came over to get him back. It became that we would scan the field for large dogs off leads in case they came over to her. What always amazed me was the stupidity or arrogance of some dog owners who knew their dog was difficult to control but would still let them off their lead. One dog Sam did take to was a large and playful Weimeraner called Oscar. We met him and his owner over the park the spring after Sam came to us. He was still young but already a lump of a dog; Oscar was beautiful, with a ghost-grey shiny coat and a very large personality to boot. He sniffed Sam and Sam sniffed back and that was that. Theirs was a nodding friendship which was fine for both of them. Sam would stand and watch as Oscar's owner threw a ball and Oscar would retrieve it. Despite Sam's fear of other dogs, she was never frightened of Weimeraners as she thought they were all as daft and soft as Oscar.

We had conquered Sam's car sickness (with tablets) so the next thing to tackle was her fear of dogs. What we needed was a way she could meet dogs of all shapes and sizes under controlled conditions. I knew someone who ran a dog training class in the next village, only a five minute car journey away, close enough not to need any medication. Sam already knew how to sit and to lie down (which she found easier and more comfortable), she would stay and then come to me (after a fashion) but what she needed was to meet other dogs and socialise. The kennels that Sam went to said she was fine with other dogs so maybe it was us. Either way, we could all do with some training.

The classes were run in a community hall. When we arrived there was no-one outside so we opened the side door and took Sam in. She was very wary but followed me. I think at first she registered the people (she loved people) and then she saw other dogs (not so sure of dogs). We picked a spot across the room beside a Border collie puppy and a large Rottweiler bitch. Sam sat and watched the other dogs, very tense, very wary. After a little while she let the collie sniff her, and the Rottweiler. She even sniffed them in turn. We did some simple sits and stays but Sam was a bit awed by everyone and was having problems sitting on the parquet floor. We watched some of the others in the class and were amazed. One little girl had a miniature Schnauzer that would sit, stay, and walk in a circle up and down the room so beautifully. Sam relaxed even more, and lay down on her side and watched the dogs with a bored easiness. The thing she raised her ears for was the sit and recall. Here the dog would sit, the owner would walk the other end of the hall and then call them. The dog would run up the hall and then sit right in front of them, with their heads and chins up against the owner's bellies. This was called a "present" (as in arms, not Christmas).

Even Chalkie the Labrador retriever did the present. He was probably the unofficial star of the class, a large 4 year old Labrador, a big lump of golden dopiness. He was lovely but his reluctance to actually obey Helen, his owner, was incorrigible. He had been a rescue as he was abandoned as untrainable. Helen had taken him in as a project and had been bringing him to dog training class for some time where he was making great strides – but mostly to get a laugh! Helen would walk Chalkie out to the centre of the floor when asked and he would walk with her, smiling broadly and tail wagging from side to side like a hug hairy scythe. He would sit and look up at her as Helen commanded him to "Sit" and "Chalkie – stay!" Helen would turn, and walk ten yards up the hall. As she walked Chalkie would smile again and scan his audience as if to say, "Watch this, everyone". Helen would only have gone five yards and he would be up and following, quietly behind her, tail still swiping the air. The audience reaction was what Chalkie loved and Helen would turn and he would be standing right beside her, still grinning broadly. Helen would remonstrate with him and take him back to his spot and the same routine would happen. No matter how much Helen would chide him, Chalkie would just grin at her with a soppy loving Labrador smile. "Oh Chalkie, we've been coming here for over a year….." Chalkie would play the crowd a few times, and then he would get it right, just to prove to everyone that he did know what to do and could if he wanted. He just wanted to make everyone as happy as he was!

The first time Sam took to the floor was to do a circuit of the room, in front of the other dogs to see how she would react and to build up her confidence. Initially she was hesitant, but then I took a small handful of chopped frankfurter and held some above her nose. This was the business! She trotted around the room and everyone was so taken with her – people were saying how pretty the little black greyhound was, and as we went she began to raise her feet more, so that in the end she was trotting like a Lipizzaner horse at the Spanish Riding School!

I had taught her to sit but the parquet floor was difficult to get a good purchase on so she preferred to lie down, which was fine - after all, we were not there for obedience but for socialising. After a few weeks she grasped the recall and she would lie down as I walked away, and watch me, waiting to be called. Then she would fly up the room, feet slipping a bit but focussed on getting to me. I don't remember when it actually happened but there was almost a cheer the day she did it – she came up to me, stopped in front of me, tight to me, chin on my tummy, looking up into my face. Carolyn (one of the trainers) announced that she was the only greyhound that she had ever seen do a proper "present"!

She learned to do the sit and stay (well, lie down and stay) for up to ten minutes, even on the evening that two of the dogs decided to have a scuffle. Sam just lay there watching me as a war began around her. What a star!

She really enjoyed her Wednesday evening trips to dog class. Reaching for the car keys and a mention of "Right then, dog class" would initiate a bouncing black ball of fur as she flew round the room in excitement. She would be in the car like a shot with her lead, coat, poop scoop bags and a large bag of chopped up smoked sausage!

On our walks across the cricket pitch in the mornings we would usually bump into a Norfolk terrier called Max and a hyperactive tennis-ball obsessed Spaniel called Sam. Our Sam never knew what to make of either of these but she was not too frightened. Armelle was taking Sam around the pitch one afternoon when she bumped into Sam and his owner, Lynne. Sam the Spaniel was really keen for our Sam to play with him and kept nudging her and dropping his tennis ball at her feet. Our Sammy studiously ignored him so he got more and more frustrated as she refused to play. He eventually huffed and walked off taking his tennis ball with him.   Sam stopped heading up the road to the pitch in the mornings but instead wanted to walk the other way through the estate. In the afternoons or evenings she was perfectly happy to go any direction. We even walked home once or twice with "The Krays" – a pair of psychotic Bichon Frisee's who now seemed to accept Sam and allowed her to come along with them.

The Accident

On a couple of walks across the pitch we bumped into Ben, a stocky Labrador whose owner lived a few doors down from us. He was a rescue dog from an animal shelter. He was very aggressive with other dogs and had to be kept on a leash. We had come practically face to face on a number of walks but generally we kept well out his way. This particular warm September Sunday we had enjoyed a long walk up the canal in the morning and pottered in the garden all afternoon. Sam had lain out on the lawn or on her bed in the sun in front of the patio doors. After tea I said to Armelle that I would take Sam out, though she did not really need a walk. I put Sam on her lead and we went down the road towards the pitch. We walked onto the pitch and Sam walked ahead, on her extendable lead. As we headed towards the area behind the gardens I could see our neighbour coming towards me. Then I saw Ben. He was off his lead.

I froze and started to reel Sam towards me but it was too late – Ben flew at us, growling and barking. He ran at Sam and she tried to pull away. I grabbed Ben but he pulled out of my grasp and again tried to bite Sam. Again I held him by the collar and hung on to him as I wrestled on the floor with him. Sam was terrified and ran to the full length of the extendable lead (20 feet) and stopped with a jolt, then wriggled out of the collar and ran. My neighbour came over and apologised and took Ben back, put him back on his lead. I was more concerned about what had happened to Sam. She was trotting up and down, looking dazed and frightened. I called her name, and told her to "Wait". This was where the dog classes really worked, as she stopped and waited for me to come to her. I checked her over, there seemed to be no injuries, I put her collar on and we continued her walk. I wanted her to settle down, and she did. Half way back Armelle came to find us as our neighbour had knocked and told her Sam had run off. That evening we all sat on the bed watching TV and I put Sam to bed as normal.

The next morning Sam had problems eating her breakfast, so I rang the vets and took her down that morning. I explained what had happened and the vet examined her. There was nothing visibly wrong, she put it down to the collar (a 1 ½ inch webbing martingale) rubbing her throat and bruising it. Sam had a jab, some painkillers and I took her home. That afternoon I was on a speed awareness course (long story...). When I came home, Sam was fine – she had eaten her breakfast dinnertime and was now waiting for her tea. We gave her something lighter – rice and vegetables. After her first mouthful she started to cry. The crying got worse; she was evidently in pain and getting more and more distressed. I rang the vets, and they said to take her down. Armelle went up to change as I got Sam's lead and coat. In the five minutes it took Armelle to get ready, Sam's throat started to swell up. She was having problems breathing too. We got her in the back of the car and I flew down through Swansea to the vets. I got Sammy out and we walked her in. By now she was really distressed. Gareth, the duty vet, looked at her and said it was internal bleeding but they would try and staunch it, and maybe do a tracheotomy to relieve the breathing problem. She would be ok. We left her and drove home, shell-shocked. Before leaving Sam I held her and promised her that as soon as she was better we would go for a trip in the van together.

We had not been home long before the Vets rang. Sam had collapsed practically as soon as we had left her. She had stopped breathing but they had resuscitated her and she was on a drip. Gareth was not sure how she would do, but they would have to do the tracheotomy immediately. He felt that if she could get air down her then that would be the biggest problem; they would staunch the bleeding whilst they were in there putting in the airway.

About 1 o'clock the vets rang us back to say that the tracheotomy had gone well, they had put pads on the bleeding and that Sam seemed settled. We could go down to see her if we wished. As she seemed to be ok and was resting, we decided to let her get some sleep and that we would pop down in the morning. Relieved, Armelle and I went to bed and had a very fitful sleep.

It was about six o'clock that we were wakened by the phone ringing - it was Ellie, the duty nurse at the vets. Sammy had started bleeding again in the night and they could not stop

111

it – the bleeding was from too may points, and as she was so weak she just could not fight any longer and had passed away. Little Sammy, everyone's friend, had died, killed by her greatest fear – attacked by another dog.

We were shell-shocked, upset and angry. That morning we called on our neighbours to tell them about what had happened. They had already decided to send Ben back to the animal shelter. My neighbour was also very upset, and he admitted that he was not able to walk Ben on a lead as he had pulled him and his daughter over as he was so strong. So he had walked an aggressive dog on the pitch without a lead.

I learned two things with Sam's death. Firstly, extendable leads and martingales are a potentially dangerous combination for a greyhound. Secondly, how overconfident and (largely unintentionally) irresponsible people can be walking an uncontrolled dog off its lead. One stupid action ended up upsetting two families and it was all so bloody needless. I wrote to the Dogs Trust to let them know what had happened to see if they would publish a letter in their magazine about dogs off leads, and I wrote to the Local

Authority about the enforcement of lead wearing. Unfortunately though both parties were very sympathetic thay said that there was nothing that they could do, and no letter was ever published

Sam was cremated like Sal had been, but this time we decided to scatter her ashes in one of her favourite places.   She had one last trip in the van; we took her up to Dinefwr Park and scattered her amongst the bluebells in Castle Wood. We had taken a lovely photo of her there in the spring, standing in the midst of the blue flowers, smiling and doing her best "Come on, you two," look. The freaky thing had been that the scatter-tube her ashes had come in had a lovely picture on the tube – of a bluebell wood. Was the White Dog still looking over her after all? Now there would be two of them to watch over us.

We were even more upset over losing our Sammy. It had been so sudden. It was also so uncalled for, and could have been averted. I blamed myself (and probably always will) for taking her out that night and going over the pitch. Armelle had a feeling that we should not have gone, and blamed herself for not stopping us. My Mum was very upset as she had come back from

113

a break with my sister to find us grieving for Sam, and she grieved too. No more would Sammy run across the landing and jump onto Nan's bed for a cuddle and a piece of toast. We had only had Sam two and a half years, and she died three days short of her fifth birthday. It seemed to me that she had never been given a proper chance.

The Foster from Gloucester

Once again we were in that limbo period, grieving but longing for another dog as well. We decided that we would not rush in but maybe we would try another foster. We had 12 years of greyhound experience by now, of different dogs with their foibles and problems. The other thing with a foster was that there was no permanent commitment, but an offer to assess the dog, find out their issues, their particular needs, and then pass them on to someone who can best meet those needs. We approached another greyhound rescue centre and asked about taking a dog on. We told them we were looking for a 2-3 year old small greyhound bitch, quiet, with no separation issues (preferably). Though there were dogs and bitches on the website, we were persuaded that a dog would be equally as affectionate and homely as a bitch so we agreed to give a greyhound dog a go. On the way to Gloucestershire we collected a pair of greyhounds just off the boat from Ireland; both were black, a large male and a smaller female. They climbed into the hatchback of the

Picasso and settled down. We did not hear a peep from them all the way to Gloucestershire. Once at our destination we unloaded our Irish passengers and went to meet our prospective foster. There were two male dogs there, both tall; one was a brown brindle and the other black. We walked with both dogs and were content that the brindle would be the better one for us. His name was Rhys. So, we went home to think and agreed by phone a day or so later that we would come back the following week to pick him up. Rhys was not small, but he was very slight because he was so very thin; like a brindle toast-rack, his ribs showed pitifully. He was off his food as he really did not like it in kennels. A few weeks with us should give us a chance to assess him and feed him up. He had been tested in a home for a weekend and was quiet and non-destructive, though he had tried to "counter-surf" in the kitchen but had stopped when told off. When we walked him we noticed that both these dogs could not wee correctly and ended up peeing on their front feet! This was presumably due to their being so thin that nothing pointed the right way. Here we were with a 4 year old, tall (but bony) greyhound dog. Not entirely as planned but what the heck!

We had only driven for 20 minutes before Rhys had tried climbing over the seat from the hatchback into the rear seat of the car. Armelle moved to the back and spent the rest of the journey trying to persuade him to stay in the hatch. When we got home we settled him in the kitchen with his bed, bowls and everything. Rhys seemed happy with his crate and was happy to be fed in it. He walked well on the lead and was quite easy to walk, so we took him up to the local park and then later over the pitch. Again he peed on his front feet whenever he tried to mark. Importantly though, he was very friendly with children and adults and fine with the large dogs we encountered.

That evening we settled Rhys in his bed; he cried once, but then slept the rest of the night. When I got up in the morning he was clean and after breakfast I got back into the "normal routine". Rhys came with me around the cricket pitch and then out past the Sheltered Housing. Here we bumped into Lynette with Sam the Spaniel and Tarquin the Chihuahua. Rhys was ok with Sam but then he saw Tarquin; he lurched at him. Luckily I caught the pull forward and yanked him back. He was rigid and shaking with excitement. This was not very good news. Now I realised why the rescue group requested that the dogs were muzzled when out walking. I was shaken by this, as I did not expect it (maybe I was a bit naïve here). Over the next few weeks we encountered a number of small dogs and Rhys was always the same though this time he was muzzled. I had walked many greyhounds, many of them keen too (Sal was a devil for cats and squirrels, and a big dog too) but Rhys was another step up again. After what had happened to Sammy, I was unhappy that I was going to be the owner of a dog that people avoided. Sam had been attacked; now I had a dog that attacked others.

The second night Rhys cried. I went down after twenty minutes or so just to check he was ok. I went back upstairs and he cried and began to howl. I went down, but this time I sat in the kitchen until he settled, then went upstairs. Again he howled. I went down this time and sat in the living room where he could see me. He settled, but then began to cry and then howl. That was it –

the neighbours might complain. I opened the crate and fell asleep on the settee in the living room. Rhys climbed on the settee at my feet and slept like a log.

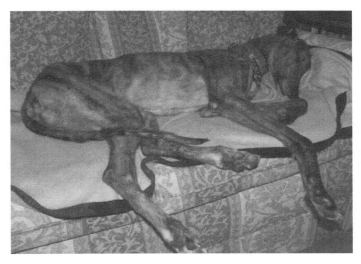

The next day we tried leaving him in his crate for ten minutes whilst we went around the house with a view to slowly increasing the times over a few weeks. He was ok with this. Within a few days we had extended this to 30 minutes or so. When we left the house for any extended periods for these first days he came with us in the car. My Mum was in hospital at this time so we would park outside the window of my Mum's room and look out at Rhys. He was a handsome boy, despite the ribs showing (he looked like a hairy xylophone). Mum could see him when he stood up to turn around. On the third trip I had to go out to the car; Rhys the escaper had climbed over the back seat then over the passenger's seat only to get himself wedged between the passenger seat and the door jamb! I had to lift his back end and pull him over the seat. All the while Rhys smiled and tried to kiss me! Softy or what!

Armelle and I had talked a lot during these first days and had come to a decision; Rhys was not a permanent dog for us – the attempt to eat Tarquin was too much of a black moment for us. We had decided that Rhys would be a foster and would have to go back. However, during the weeks we would have him we would give him a thorough assessment, work out what he really needed and show him a really good time. This is what a real home could be like.

He had continued the counter-surfing he had started in his last test-home. I told him off, but the lure of food was too much again. I even tried using the pet protector spray to make a noise as a deterrent but this did not always work. One evening whilst I was taking something into the living room and Armelle was upstairs I heard a crash as Rhys had leant up on the cooker and tried to pull down the hot frying pan of liver and onions. Fortunately he had only caught the lid and knocked that on the floor!

He was a real starver and would eat everything put in front of him. He never seemed to put on weight either. When we weighed Rhys at our vets he was 24 kilos; his racing weight had been 31 kilos. Though Armelle could walk him at his current weight, I was unsure how she would cope when he got back to 30kilos. We wormed Rhys and he did have worms but despite the worming and the huge appetite, he still stayed thin. It reminded me of my Grandfather's saying that you could not fatten a greyhound (he never saw Sally!).

The evening routine had changed now that we had decided Rhys's fate. I could not sleep on the settee for months, so instead Rhys came up to bed with us. He would climb onto the big bed to settle in between us where he would be fast asleep in no time at all; we would not hear a peep out of him all night. The first thing I would hear

121

about seven o'clock each morning was a whooshing sound as he slid off the bed and he would be there, shaking his head, bolt upright and ready for whatever the day threw at him. What was for breakfast today, then?

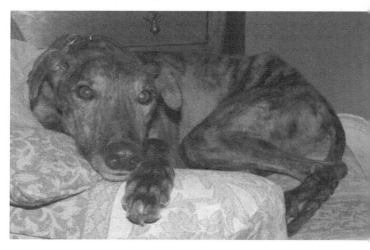

After a week he was settling in his crate for 45 minutes; we would find him calm and settled, any chews eaten. Like a big bony angel. When we came in, everything would be quiet. nothing out of place.. This particular day we had left Rhys in his crate to make an hours visit to the hospital. When we got home the house was silent (apart from Sally's radio playing) and when I walked into the kitchen Rhys smiled back at me from inside the crate. He looked out through the crate door…or rather, the hole left where Rhys had bent the door backwards. Rhys had used his strength to pull and push and buckle the door trying to get out of the heavy metal crate. He was intact, apart from a huge scratch across the bridge of his nose. Rhys tried to get out but I had a heck of a job to bend the door straight before it would open. He came out, stretching, huge bony tail wagging wildly. Rhys really liked company and did not like being on his own. At all.

Rhys had gone for other dogs over the next few weeks; usually small dogs but once or twice spaniel size too. I spoke to the Trainer from Sam's dog class and we discussed Rhys's problems. She understood why it was difficult for us to keep Rhys. She also suggested that Rhys's separation anxiety could mean that he really needed the company of another dog. Even his tester home had had another dog there.

I rang the Rescue Group and explained everything that had happened and that Rhys was not for us. It was the aggression to other dogs that really upset us most, but the separation anxiety was not fair on Rhys – he liked company

123

so should have a canine companion at the very least. At first they suggested we spoke to an animal behaviourist, which we did. However, everything the behaviourist suggested we had tried (such as crate training, leaving him gradually for longer periods) and after all, we had been through this a number of times before. I was also concerned that his not putting weight on might be indicative of liver or other digestive troubles. We took Rhys back and though we were sad, there were no tears like we had with Queenie. We were able to hand over a proper assessment paper listing his good and bad points, and what we felt he needed in a permanent home. Rhys went eventually to a home with children and another dog and I am sure he made them an absolutely fabulous pet. Whoever has him, give him a cuddle for us! And watch out, as he pees on his feet.

Little Lizzie

Three or four months after Rhys I had an e-mail from the Rescue Centre that Sam had come from; would we be interested in fostering and assessing a quiet little greyhound bitch? Lizzie needed a quiet home to see how she would cope. We were e-mailed a picture of her, a pretty brindle and white greyhound bitch, small, with her ears clamped straight along her head and tail tucked tightly between her legs, looking very uncomfortable to say the least. We went to collect her the week after. It was odd sitting in the same kitchen where we had met Sammy those years before, discussing Lizzie's background. She was a 2 year old Irish dog that had raced on the Ystrad Mynach track but had come to the centre from the track. She was very quiet and needed to be brought out of herself, but basically to see how she would cope in a normal household. It was nice that someone thought our household was a normal one. When Lizzie was brought to meet us outside, she was ever so fearful of us. I slipped the collar and lead over her head and walked her around the garden. At first she was so reluctant to move but gradually she relaxed and got intro the rhythm as we continued around the lawn. She hopped into the boot without an issue and so we waved goodbye and drove the little bundle of quiet nervousness home.

She got out of the car and came into the house, then went through to the garden. She was a bit overwhelmed when she tip-toed out onto the lawn but still managed a poo. She was very shy and that evening she did not leave her bed in the kitchen though she interacted well with us whenever we went in and out. The kitchen door was open and she was not crated. We felt that Lizzie would find a crate too oppressive, we would have to be very gentle with her. After a couple of days she started to come into the living room as far as the settee but any strange noise would send her running back to her bed. She was good as gold at night – I would settle her in her bed about ten o'clock and she would be quiet until the next morning when I got up at six to let her out. She was very clean and never had an accident in the house.

After a few days Lizzie started to become more and more reluctant to go out to the garden. We tried to bribe and encourage her but it would not work. If we got her to start to come down the garden, at the merest noise she would run back indoors. She was terrified of any strange sound. On one of her painfully slow walks down the garden path she heard the children next door and that was it – she shot up the garden and sat quivering in her bed.

Getting her out for a walk was initially fine but over the course of the first fortnight Lizzie started to get more and more difficult to get out the door. Firstly she started to not want to go out via the back door; so we tried to be positive and walk with her and encourage her which worked at first then began to be more difficult. You could not pull her, as this would only reinforce her fear and possibly hurt her. She then refused to get out of her bed for a walk or go out the garden. I tried putting her lead on in her bed and the first few times she got up. This was rewarded by chunks of smoked sausage (Sammy's favourite dog-training treat). When she refused to move at all, we lay a trail of sausage into the utility room so that when she was up following the trail I could clip on the lead and away we would go. Once she was in the utility room heading towards the door she would be fine. Once more, after a few weeks this too became a mental barrier. Plan C – we would try through the living room and front door. By now (about 6 weeks) she was settling in the living room and was more used to the telly. She would watch it, sometimes warily, and if there was the sound of children she would get up and run back to her bed. The sound of children was a real issue for her. Cue the trail of sausages to the front door which had worked but now began to get more and more problematic. It was taking up to half an hour to get her as far as the door and then out.

Once outside there were another series of mental barriers for her. Lizzie loved other dogs, big and small, and was quite gentle. People were a worry to her and she would even step into the road to avoid people coming towards us. She once pulled Armelle into the road to get away from someone walking past. If there was someone with a dog, she was better, and would even (occasionally) allow the dog-walker to stroke her.

If she saw or heard children, Lizzie would stiffen, then pull away or weave from side to side and try and hide behind our legs.   On one occasion she saw two young children of about 6 or 7 a couple of hundred yards away on the other side of the road and she started to weave uncontrollably. She would not cry, or bite or growl, just try and hide – if she had got her collar off I am sure she would have just run away.

Armelle and I tried to keep positive and be patient though it was very frustrating. Once again I was amazed at how patient I could be. Sarah from the Rescue Centre came to see Lizzie after a few weeks or so and she managed to get Lizzie out onto the back lawn. Be firm, take her out and do a few circuits and if she does not go to the loo, come back in, and then repeat. This I did, but Liz would just circuit the lawn looking stressed, not sniffing, and with no attempt to pee. Once she did, and I rewarded her with the obligatory piece of frankfurter. Sarah suggested that her fear might have been from her days in Ireland where sometimes kids throw stones at the dogs when they are being walked. I was sure that she had been kept in a shed where she had heard kids

129

playing but had never known what the noise was and so it frightened her.

We kept in touch with the Rescue Centre from the beginning, and even got advice from the dog-trainer and from other friends in Greyhound Rescue. We considered taking her to dog class to meet the children there in a controlled environment. Maybe? We remained very positive, despite the hiccoughs, that Lizzie needed a bit more time. Sarah had spoken to Armelle at the end of the first fortnight and suggested that Lizzie could go back at that stage; we declined and asked if we could try a bit longer. We had already overcome some barriers; maybe the others would come down. Sarah told Armelle that she was not sure whether Lizzie would ever cope in a home which was why she was trying her with us. She believed we would have the patience to assess her fairly.

We kept at it, as there were so many positives; she was clean, quiet, well behaved, non-destructive and a good traveller. One Sunday morning we took her in the car down to Swansea and walked her in Singleton Park and she was ok with the few pedestrians she met, a bit nervous but ok. Once again though, when we got to the Park itself she saw and heard children, someone went past on a bike and there were more people.

She was so wary. We did what we usually did, just corrected her slightly on the lead and continued, head up, in a firm and positive manner. We knew from experience and dog training that we should not reassure her as such, just keep going as if nothing special was happening. Lizzie coped quite well and we got a good buzz from that session. When we got to my Mum's nursing home we did not attempt to take Lizzie in, as we were not sure how she would cope in a confined space

with the residents. She was still too timid of
people for that.

Lizzie was another dog that enjoyed her
food and, like Sammy, she chewed every morsel.
Her teeth were (again, like Sammy) perfect little
ivory-white shiny specimens, not a hint of gingivitis
to be seen. Her digestive system was also
immaculate. She was not a raw veg. doggy like
Sally but she did like to chew. We had bought
Sam a plastic chew (supposedly chicken flavour!)
but she never really chewed it much. Rhys was
the same. Lizzie, on the other hand, discovered
the chew and proceeded to demolish it. She really
loved to give the chew a good going over and
maybe it was her way of grinding away her
frustrations. Go, Lizzie, go!

Things went on and on over the next month gradually going one step forward, two steps back, getting a bit worse each week. Lizzie was becoming more and more difficult to get out the door. Armelle had joked about us having an agoraphobic dog but it now appeared to be becoming true! We had thought of taking her to dog club but how the heck would we get her there? The trail of sausages was working less and less, pulling her in a firm and supportive way also getting harder. It was taking me up to 20 minutes to get her out the door for her morning walk. Once out the door onto the driveway she was usually fine, keeping up Sammy's morning

133

routine of a walk up the estate. During the afternoon Armelle would take her the other way over the pitch, trying to keep her eyes peeled for children. One Saturday we spent ten minutes getting Lizzie to the door and out onto the drive. We walked past the motorhome, and someone walked past the gateposts and stopped to say hello. Lizzie pulled backwards down the drive and stood facing outwards with her backside pushed tightly against the front door. Her eyes were wide with fear. After the neighbour left we coaxed Lizzie away from the doorway and she continued her walk down the estate. That was the afternoon she saw the two children a couple of hundred yards away that freaked her out. We got home and for the first time we were demoralised. I spoke to Sarah that afternoon and she told us that we had done as much as we could; it was time to pass Lizzie on. We mulled it over for a couple of days but realised that Sarah was right. Lizzie's needs were;

- A home with peace and quiet and no children
- Maybe another dog for company
- A big garden to wander in and out

- Perhaps in the country where there were fewer people

On the Tuesday, Sarah came and collected Lizzie. We were very sad but also glad again that we could have assessed her. It's been a while since she left but we still think fondly of her. We gave Sarah her chew to take with her and her lovely housecollar which suited her so beautifully. Of all our dogs, Lizzie was the prettiest. As Sarah collected her she reassured Armelle and I that we had done a good piece of work with Lizzie and that she had a better idea now of what she needed. Most importantly, she asked us to keep fostering as it was difficult to find anyone with the skills an experience that we had.

The Future?

It's been a little while now since Lizzie left; we have been on a break, originally until our summer holidays were over but due to unforeseen circumstances they were delayed until September. In October we will contact Sarah and see whether there is another dog we can help.

We have heard that Lizzie went backwards at her next foster, then improved and became a bit more confident. She is now with another family in her forever home. Again, she will go backwards a bit but the return to normality should be quicker as her self assurance builds. I look forward to the day we bump into this gorgeous little white and brindle greyhound girl, brimming with confidence!

Fostering has its ups and downs, and training can be a bit of a challenge. Fosters, like Rhys and Lizzie, may be short-term or they could be like Sammy, and find with us a forever home. Either way, we keep our eyes open and are waiting again for the time we have another Hound in the House.

Excerpt from "Found a Penny (or 49 ½ Shades of Greyhound)"

Being without a dog was a strange time; it was nice in some ways, in that we could come and go as we pleased, make our craft items and leave paint and brushes, or jam jars and fruit everywhere, could have lie in's when we wanted. In short it allowed us to be totally selfish. Being able to eat all a meal and not having to leave a bit. But it was also not so nice. Coming home to an empty house, lacking any sort of routine, even the loose one we used to have. The worst of all was the lack of someone to nurture.

After the fosters we were a bit wary, maybe even bruised, in that we had self doubts that we would never find the right dog again. Sally and Sam had been so very special and the others though special had been broken in various degrees. How we ended up with the next dog was a bit of a coincidence.

I returned to work after being on leave to find an e-mail from a colleague in another section of the council. He had found a lurcher wandering on the beach in Port Talbot and with some others wanted to get it caught safely and looked after. The local pound would take the dog but there was always the fear that if not claimed the dog would be put down. Rich (my colleague) contacted me as he had heard that I had links with some greyhound charities. So, I contacted Sarah at the rescue kennels and discussed how to get the dog captured and then rehomed.

Before we could put any plan into action, Rich called to see me and he told me that the lady who had first seen the lurcher had managed to feed him, get a lead on him and take him home. After considering getting him to the rescue kennels she decided that he fitted in so would keep him.

I e-mailed Sarah to let her know that the great plan would not be required. Sarah's reply asked us whether Armelle and I wanted to do a bit of fostering again, and that she had a few dogs in. There were three black dogs, notoriously difficult to rehome as they were not as pretty as the other colours. One had been brought in by a trainer, one arrived from Ireland and the other handed in by a farmer. They were all around 3-4 years old. Have a think – no pressure.

Armelle and I pondered things over for a while but we had had our holidays, most of the craft fairs were over for the summer so it might be a good time to give the dogs ago. Even if for a month or so, it would be a nice distraction. I contacted Sarah and let her know we could pop over on the Friday afternoon as I was off work so we could see the prospective fosters.

We had a chat with Sarah and she said she thought that one of the dogs would be a better fit than the rest; she had been found wandering in a field in Mid Wales and taken in by the Farmer who had found her. He looked after her for a few days until the Greyhound Rescue Charity collected her and so she ended up with Sarah. Armelle and I were open to whatever she thought was best so Sarah disappeared and came back with a tall black greyhound on a blue lead. Her coat was rough but with a slight shine, she was thin but her eyes were bright and had that sparkle. The dog had no name as she had been found wandering. She was very affectionate and came over immediately for a cuddle from both Armelle and myself. Sarah brought out her small terrier which the new dog took very little notice of. Again, a good sign. We walked the dog around the paddock where she came with us confidently with a brightness which belied the fact we had never met before. She really loved people. When we got back to the courtyard I explained that we had a couple of craft shows so could not collect her until the following weekend. Sarah agreed but if we were not keen, if someone else wanted her then she could go with them. I looked down into the greyhound's deep brown eyes – no, I said, keep her for us, we'll give her a chance.

Armelle and I were quite excited as we drove home, and thinking about what we needed to get and when would be best to collect her. Sarah had called the dog Susie, which really did not suit her. I suggested Poppy, but black poppy was not right. Armelle chimed up with "What about Penny – like the Penny Black stamp?" So we might not have had the dog yet, but we had a name. Penny.

Excerpt from "Found a Penny" copyright Crafty Dog Books, 2013. Due out 2014.